Do not forget the things your eyes have seen
or let them slip from your heart as long as you live.
Teach them to your children and to their children after them.

DEUTERONOMY 4:9

When home is ruled according to God's Word,
angels might be asked to stay with us,
and they would not find themselves
out of their element.

Charles Spurgeon

The Pocket Guide for Parents: Raising Godly Kids

Copyright © 2006 by Bordon Books

Product developed by Bordon Books, Tulsa, Oklahoma

Writing and Compilation by Rebecca Currington, Patricia R. Mitchell, Noelle Roso, and Deborah Webb in association with SnapdragonGroup℠ Editorial Services.
Cover design by Thinkpen Designs.

Published by Bethany House Publishers
11400 Hampshire Avenue South
Bloomington, Minnesota 55438

Bethany House Publishers is a division of
Baker Publishing Group, Grand Rapids, Michigan.

Printed in the United States of America
ISBN-13: 978-0-7642-0223-0
ISBN-10: 0-7642-0223-5

Library of Congress Cataloging-in-Publication Data
The pocket guide for parents : raising godly kids.
        p. cm.
Summary: "This compact parenting book offers practical help and advises parents on fostering love and respect among family members as well as helps them understand their children's points of view"—Provided by publisher.
        ISBN 0-7642-0223-5 (pbk.)
1. Parenting—Religious aspects—Christianity. I. Bethany House Publishers.
        BV4529.P63 2006
        248.8'45–dc22   2006010049

THE POCKET GUIDE for PARENTS

Raising Godly Kids

BETHANYHOUSE

MINNEAPOLIS, MINNESOTA

Introduction

Your children are on loan to you from God. He's depending on you to teach them by principle and precept how to walk in relationship with Him. It's a tremendous task, but one that God does not expect you to accomplish alone. He's promised to work with you, providing you with wisdom and understanding, inspiration and instruction, everything you need to succeed in your effort to produce citizens for His kingdom.

The Pocket Parent: A Guide to Raising Godly Kids offers you a two-pronged strategy. First, you will find inspiration and instruction aimed at helping you establish your own life in the things of God. The best way to raise godly kids is to be a godly parent. Second, this important little book will help you better understand your children and the most effective ways to instill in them important God-centered principles and precepts.

God is faithful! He's completely able to help you raise your children to be people of faith, strong and settled in character and beliefs. Depend on Him—He's depending on you!

Contents

III. Parenting Pitfalls

IV. Gems for Your Journey

**All your children will have God for their teacher—
what a mentor for your children!**

Secrets for Becoming a Godly Parent

[God's] divine power has given us everything needed for life and godliness, through the knowledge of him who called us by his own glory and goodness.

2 PETER 1:3 NRSV

Blueprint for Godliness
God's Plan for Becoming Godly

It's a principle in spiritual matters as it is in life: What you have not learned yourself, you cannot teach others. The primary qualification for raising godly kids is to be a godly parent. Without that, not only will you fail, but you will present a false front that is sure to send your children fleeing in the opposite direction. Children need role models in the Christian faith—genuine, open, God-fearing, God-seeking role models.

Well, you might be thinking, *I guess it's hopeless then. I'm certainly not the kind of person I want my child to be, and I don't know how to become that person.* If so, then you're on the right track. You'll never be the kind of parent you need to be without God's help, and being able to admit your inadequacy gives you a strategic advantage. No excuses, no games, no stalling, just honesty before God. You couldn't be in a better position to accomplish your goal.

> To teach is to learn twice.
> -Joseph Joubert

Titus 3:3-5 (MSG) says: "It wasn't so long ago that we ourselves were stupid and stubborn, dupes of sin, ordered every which way by our glands, going around with a chip on our shoulder, hated and hating back. But when God, our kind and loving Savior God, stepped in, he saved us from all that. It was all his doing; we had nothing to do with it. He gave us a good bath, and we came out of it new people, washed inside and out by the Holy Spirit."

To become a godly parent, you must start where we all start—by taking hold of God's amazing grace, offering up all your failings and missteps, rebellion and sin, and letting Him wash you clean with the blood of Jesus Christ that was shed for you. Ephesians 1:7 tells us: "In him [Jesus Christ] we have redemption

10

through his blood, the forgiveness of sins, in accordance with the riches of God's grace." Colossians 1:13-14 confirms that your condition, while unworthy, is made worthy in Christ. It says: "[Jesus Christ] has rescued us from the dominion of darkness and brought us into the kingdom of the Son he loves, in whom we have redemption, the forgiveness of sins."

> *To become a godly parent,*
> *you must start where we all start*
> *—by taking hold of God's*
> *amazing grace.*

11

This transaction—your blighted baggage of sin for His spotless righteousness—is remarkable in its simplicity. All you need do is ask and receive. God's miraculous, transforming power will change you from the person you were to the person your child can respect and follow down the path of godliness.

You may already have made things right between you and God. You may already be walking in His love and grace. But if you haven't, let this be your prayer:

Father God:
I know that I have broken your laws and my sins have separated me from you. I am truly sorry, and now I want to turn away from my past sinful life. Please forgive me, and help me avoid sinning again. I believe that your Son, Jesus Christ, died for my sins, was resurrected from the dead, is alive, and hears my prayer. I invite Jesus to become the Lord of my life, to rule and reign in my heart from this day forward. Please send your Holy Spirit to help me obey you and do your will.
In Jesus' name I pray,
Amen.

Now that your feet have been planted on the path of godliness, you will be able to become the godly parent and role model your child needs. But don't take your new standing with God, your new relationship with Christ, for granted. Listen to the words of the apostle Peter: "Make every effort to add to your faith goodness; and to goodness, knowledge; and to knowledge, self-control; and to self-control, perseverance; and to perseverance, godliness; and to godliness, brotherly kindness; and to brotherly kindness, love. For if you possess these qualities in increasing measure, they will keep you from being ineffective and unproductive in your knowledge of our Lord Jesus Christ" (2 Peter 1:5-8).

This is God's blueprint for spiritual growth. Upon your foundation of faith, you should add goodness—acknowledging God's goodness in your life and by the power of the Holy Spirit becoming good as He is good. To goodness, grow in your knowledge about God—studying His Word, experiencing His character, learning about His ways. To your knowledge, add self-control—choosing moment by moment a life of holiness rather than a life of selfish pursuits and gratification. To your self-control, add endurance—realizing that a godly life is a work in progress. And to your endurance, add godliness. That godliness leads to love for God, for others, and for your children. And that love is the agape kind, not the soft, indulgent love many parents feel for their kids, but the kind of love God has for us—a selfless, sacrificial, often tough love, that always seeks our eternal best.

Just as He was there with a plan to save you and set your feet on the path of godliness, God is there to help you build your spiritual structure—your soul—tall and strong on the foundation of your faith. Take His hand and listen for His voice. Day by day, you will be growing in godliness and providing a rich environment in which to grow godly kids.

A Simple Plan
Developing a Strong Personal Relationship With God

The best way to ensure that your spiritual growth is smooth and constant is to have a plan—not an exacting plan that leaves you feeling overwhelmed and inadequate, but a plan that will encourage you to keep at it. Think of it as a spiritual diet and exercise program, if you will. You can't go wrong with these ten keys to spiritual growth:

1. **Prayer.** Spend time talking to God each day—about your life, your marriage, your kids, your job. As something comes to mind, share it with Him. You don't need a tabernacle to pray, and you don't need a fancy speech to gain His attention. He is as close as your heartbeat and always available. Choose at least one time a day to give God your focused attention. This doesn't need to be an extended period, but time enough to talk—and listen—without feeling rushed.

2. **Read the Bible.** God's Word is more than a book; it's your connection to God. He has provided you with a written account of His history with the human race. Within its pages, you can learn who God is, what He has done for you, what He expects you to do for Him. It is also a beautiful and graceful expression of His love for you and intentions for you. The Bible will tell you how to live life to the fullest, how to avoid harmful, life-wasting words, behaviors, and attitudes and maximize the time you've been given here on earth.

3. **Study the lives and writings of great men and women of faith.** The fields of faith have been plowed before—why cover every inch of it again, especially when you can learn and grow through the experiences of others?

13

4. **Attend a local church.** A body of believers contains all the irritations and frustrations of any other family. Sometimes, you'll want to pack your bag and run away. But in the end, a church family provides stability, companionship, comfort, assistance, wisdom, guidance, and a sense of belonging. Annoying—sometimes, but so worth it!

5. **Become a doer.** Spiritual truth does you no good unless you are willing to put hands and feet to it. When you learn something new, venture out. See how it works. You may be taking baby steps at first, but before long that principle will become part of your lifestyle, where it can do you and those around you some good.

6. **Practice the power of positive thinking.** You may think it's cliché, but negativity will leave you lying in the dust and spiritually helpless. Of course, positive thinking in and of itself has no real power. But the idea that reprogramming your mind to believe that you can trust God to do what He says He's going to do is empowering to the max. The object of your positive thinking becomes God rather than yourself. Isn't that what we call faith?

7. **Read Christian books.** From the classic Christian writers to splendid works of inspiration, the Christian book industry provides a wealth of books to challenge, educate, and inspire you. Check it out.

8. **Keep a spiritual growth journal.** It's much easier to stay enthusiastic about your progress in the life of faith when you can see it in black and white. A journal allows you to document your spiritual journey by recalling your victories and acknowledging your mistakes.

9. **Develop a love for worship.** This sometimes daunting term simply means to express homage or reverence, adoration and devotion. That might mean lifting your voice in song with fellow worshipers or whispering your appreciation in words straight from your heart. It could even mean sitting or kneeling in silent meditation in His presence.

10. **Be thankful.** God loves to hear you say thanks just as much as you love to hear those words from your children. But being thankful has other benefits as well. It keeps you in tune with what is really important in life, helps you avoid pride and arrogance, and puts you in a right attitude to hear and understand what God is saying to you.

Caring for your spirit and soul with the same diligence you would attend to your physical health and well-being has many benefits—for you and also for your kids. Your efforts provide them with a sound role model and an appreciation for the practical aspects of faith. It's difficult to make your children respond to mere words: "I want you to be honest." "I expect you to do the right thing." But words carry a lot more weight when your kids see you walking in the principles you want to instill in them.

15

Standing in the Gap
Praying for Your Children

Far be it from me that I should sin against the LORD
by failing to pray for you.
1 SAMUEL 12:23

Every step of the way, godly parents pray for their children. Why? Because prayer is the most powerful and effective weapon they have in their battle against the designs of the devil, the world, and the flesh.

Samuel, spiritual father to God's people Israel, took very seriously his role as intercessor for the people. As Samuel retired from his office as Israel's judge, he pledged to continue to lift the people's needs and petitions to God in prayer. Not to do so, he said, would cause him to sin against God. Jesus, in His High Priestly Prayer, prayed for all God's children—not just the disciples who followed Him during His earthly ministry, but "also for those who will believe in me through their message" (John 17:20). Jesus continues as your Intercessor before your Father in heaven. He is praying for you now.

When you pray for your children, it's as if you take your heavenly Father's hand in one hand and your child's hand in the other. You perform the Christ-like work of intercession in two ways:

1. In your words of gratitude for the lives of your children, you recognize God as the Creator of all life and remind yourself of the wondrous mystery, the incalculable value, and the sacred gift God has given you as a parent.

2. In the petitions you put before God, you express your trust in His power, authority, and love. You name those things that you, as a parent, know your children need—a believing heart, a strong character, a spirit of gratitude, a godly attitude.

[Jesus said,]: "If you sinful people know how to give good gifts to your children, how much more will your heavenly Father give good gifts to those who ask him."

MATTHEW 7:11 NLT

Ask Him! God has blessed you with the gift of children. He's not deserting you now. But how? you ask. What words do I use? How do I speak to the Lord about those who are closest to my heart? Let these words inspire you:.

Heavenly Father,
Thank you for blessing me with the gift of a son/daughter. Sometimes, though, I feel overwhelmed with all the responsibilities that come with raising children. A lot of times I worry I'm not doing the right thing, and often I know I've done the wrong thing. For these times, I beg your forgiveness. Increase

in me your wisdom so I can lead those you have entrusted to me in the way of truth and light. Grant my children a willingness to welcome your Spirit at work in them. Protect them, Lord, and watch over them. Keep them free from sickness and harm—safe in your tender and affectionate care. I pray in the name of Jesus Christ, who graciously brings the prayers of believers to our Father in heaven.
Amen.

At times, words don't come easily. Perhaps your heart breaks with grief at the suffering your child must endure because of accident, injury, ill health, or disability. Your heavenly Father knows. He was there on Calvary. He knows what it's like to watch a child suffer. He knows, too, the agony you feel when you detect signs of rebelliousness or disobedience in your children. He feels it when He looks in the hardened hearts of those He yearns to call His own.

In prayer, you don't even need to use words. In his letter to the Romans, Paul writes:

The Spirit helps us in our weakness. We do not know what we ought to pray for, but the Spirit himself intercedes for us with groans that words cannot express. And he who searches our hearts knows the mind of the Spirit, because the Spirit intercedes for the saints in accordance with God's will.

ROMANS 8:26-27

You could not give your children a more valuable gift than the gift of your prayers.

First, you set for them an example. They learn from an early age to pray not only for themselves but also for others, especially those God has given them in their family. When they become parents themselves, your legacy of prayer will reach down to bless the lives of your children's children and their children.

17

Second, you instill in them knowledge—knowledge that, no matter what the day brings, they have God's care in your prayers. Whether it's a tough math test or the schoolyard bully, your children's confidence and courage stem from the assurance of your love and concern reaching out to them through the gift of your prayers.

Third, you put in front of them God's presence. When temptation comes—and it comes to everyone—your children face the certainty of answering to a godly and God-fearing parent. The promises of God you use in prayer may well be the ones that the Holy Spirit uses to remind your child of his or her identity as God's daughter or son.

The earnest prayer of a righteous person has great power and wonderful results.

JAMES 5:16 NLT

Prayer works. Prayer invites Jesus Christ to stand at the head of your family. It draws you and your children into the godly company of all believers. Daily prayer on behalf of your children is your God-given privilege and your sacred duty as a parent. Use it wisely. Use it often. Use it well.

Open Heart—Open Mind
Seeing Your Child's Point of View

Put yourself back in time a little—back to the time when you were growing up. As a child, you probably experienced fears and uncertainties that seem trivial to you now. Maybe you firmly believed a monster lurked under your bed, ready and eager to bite unprotected toes. Perhaps something your mother said rocked your little world, only to realize later you had misunderstood her remark. Or in teasing you, your brother inadvertently struck a sensitive nerve. At the time, though, he seemed like the meanest kid on the block!

A child's perspective often gives small things a larger-than-life aspect, yet his or her feelings, fears, and anxieties are real. Something heard or seen on TV news terrifies a young viewer who hasn't the ability to differentiate an isolated incident from imminent danger. An uncomfortable situation at school depresses or humiliates a student without the maturity and insight to lay blame where it belongs. The effects of a changing body—simply signs of growing up to you—can pull a child into an isolated world of self-criticism, misinformation, and embarrassment.

> **Rejoice with those who rejoice,**
> **and weep with those who weep.**
> **ROMANS 12:15 NKJV**

As adults, we know instinctively who's listening to us and who's just biding their time until they can jump in and take over the conversation. Children know, too.

Listening—active listening—shows you care about what your children really think. If you move in too soon with advice, judgment, or a solution (even if you're entirely correct in your assessment of the situation), you can effectively end your child's opportunity and desire to say any more. It's not that your child will abandon or change his perspective—not at all. It's just that he may choose not to share it with you next time.

Active listening includes verbal cues, such as "I see," "I understand," and brief comments or questions to help you grasp both the objective and subjective issues as your child sees them. Active listening expresses concern through body language. Eye contact, a gentle touch, an understanding nod, and relaxed posture encourage your child to tell you everything on his or her mind.

The first duty of love is to listen.
Learn the power behind asking questions.

Your active listening, however, doesn't mean you wholeheartedly agree with and automatically accept everything you hear. When your child has finished speaking, acknowledge his or her feelings. Review the facts as he or she has related them to you. As the parent, it's time for you to provide the benefit of your experience, insight, and counsel, as appropriate. In 1 Corinthians 13:11 (NLT), Paul says, "It's like this: When I was a child, I spoke and thought and reasoned as a child does. But when I grew up, I put away childish things."

Your children look to you for guidance as they move away from childish things. In doing so, they pick up a lot just by observing how you treat the opinions of your friends and relatives, how you react to opposing political views, and how respectfully you consider someone else's perspective. How you listen and how you respond teaches your children either to stubbornly cling to first impressions and personal feelings, or to take into account other ways of looking at things. Other views, however—even those of children—are not necessarily based on the truth.

We will hold to the truth in love,
becoming more and more in every way like Christ,
who is the head of his body, the church.

EPHESIANS 4:15 NLT

If you need time to check facts, hear other opinions, or verify some of the statements your child has made—simply say so and explain why. Tell your child you want to be fair to everyone concerned. Describe the bad consequences of jumping to conclusions.

Suggest that some things happen for reasons not readily apparent, and thoughtful people try to find out all they can before reaching a conclusion. Depending on the situation, you may want to simply say you need a little time alone to think through what you've heard before acting on it. In all this, reinforce your approval of your child's willingness to talk about it.

If you suspect your child has slanted a story, you might want to probe with leading questions. Give ample opportunity for your child to tell the truth, even if the truth reveals guilt or puts him or her in an unfavorable light. As Christ has forgiven you, assure your child of your forgiveness. Then, determine what needs to be done, what reparations need to be made, or what kind of follow-up needs to take place. Empathize with your child's perspective, but clearly describe the behavior you desire. This might be a good time to pray with your child.

21

**A word aptly spoken is like apples of gold
in settings of silver.**

PROVERBS 25:11

Open-mindedness allows for thoughtful discussion and evaluation of many and varied points of view, including those of children. Lead conversations about the pros and cons of differing perspectives. While not suggesting that all opinions are equally respectable (they're not), give your children a method they can use to identify faulty thinking. In religious matters, cite the Bible as the standard by which you measure your values and principles. In other matters, talk about the things that are important to you and how you have reached the conclusions you have reached.

Your godly response to your children's disclosures says volumes about your compassion and willingness to hear what others think, feel, and believe. It models for your children the saintly art of listening—with love.

As for the toe-nibbling monster lurking under the bed—it's best to take a peek. You just never know.

Encouraging Words
Motivating and Encouraging Your Children

**Lift up the hands which hang down,
and the feeble knees.**

HEBREWS 12:12 KJV

The prophet Elijah sat down under a tree and told the Lord he had had enough of life. He declared himself the only one left who believed in the Lord God and lived according to His covenant. Despite his fiery sermons, God's idolatrous people failed to repent of their sins and walk according to His Commandments. In addition, King Ahab and Queen Jezebel pursued the prophet to kill him. Elijah, discouraged and fearful, went out into the desert and lay down to sleep with no desire to wake up again.

God didn't allow Elijah to wallow in self-pity, but neither did He simply order him to buck up. Our compassionate God sent an angel to provide Elijah with food and drink—not once, but twice. Our merciful Lord appeared to Elijah and spoke to him in a still, small voice. The Lord assured Elijah he was not the last remaining godly man on earth, and he yet had work to do. With the Lord's words of encouragement fresh in his ears, Elijah resumed his work as prophet in the kingdom of God (See 1 Kings 19:18).

When life gets you down, to whom do you turn? Scripture bids us to turn to God, who promises to hear, encourage, and guide us when we think we just can't go on any longer.

**Cast all your anxiety on him
because he cares for you.**

1 PETER 5:7

When your children feel anxious, they bring their cares to you.

You may or may not know why your child is feeling discouraged. If you believe you know, let your child confirm your suspicions. He or she may add details or twists of which you're unaware. If you don't know the reason, invite your child to talk to you. Find a quiet and private place. Say you notice he seems a little down in the dumps today, you see she seems to have something on her mind. You might get "nothing" for an answer. Use the opportunity to assure your child you're available any time he or she would like to talk, then revisit the subject again if the mood persists. Barring a deep-seated emotional problem, you should be able to learn the cause of your child's low spirits.

Safe, for a child,
is his father's hand, holding him tight.

Once you and your child identify what's wrong, a solution usually isn't far behind. If he fears failure on a project or an assignment, encourage him with words and with action. "You can do it!" rings hollow if not backed up with clear, practical ideas on how to do it. If she finds herself snubbed by her classmates, simply saying "It's just a part of growing up" may have some truth to it, but it's not much of an uplifting message. She might benefit from your help in talking about her value in your eyes—and God's.

Your child's temporary frustration over schoolwork, friends, personal appearance, mental aptitude, physical prowess, or natural abilities gives you a golden opportunity to instill godly values.

Here are a few examples:

★ Discouragement stemming from comparison between self and others easily leads to discussions of what constitutes true worth and character.

★ Discouragement after not performing to expectations of self or others can result in a talk about setting realistic expectations, the value of working hard and doing one's best, and your love and pride in your child for being who he is.

★ Discouragement in the face of an upcoming assignment, project, or test allows you to explain the importance of the task at hand, perhaps even offering a time when you feared, but faced, a similar challenge.

While a heart-to-heart pep talk may do the trick, you might take note of the problem that causes anxiety in the life of your child. Maybe the promise of a reward upon the completion of a task would give your child something to look forward to. Perhaps you could demonstrate how to break down a dreaded task into smaller bits so it's less formidable. Or you could set up and celebrate small goals so your child can recognize progress. For less tangible causes—self-doubt, feelings of inadequacy, inner fears—you might want to enlist the help of your minister, your child's teachers, or other significant adults. Privately share with them your child's recurrent feelings of personal discouragement and ask them to praise him or her when praise is due. Look for opportunities to point out his successes, her talents.

If God is for us, who can be against us?
ROMANS 8:31

Everyone gets discouraged from time to time. But as Elijah found out, God neither wishes nor desires His people to walk off the job. Instead, He says, "Come to Me." He is our Source of refreshment, support, encouragement, and motivation. Get yours from Him. Then give of what He has so graciously given to you.

Love Means Forever
Showing Your Children Unconditional Love

God is love.

1 JOHN 4:8 KJV

Because of who He is, God loves His children. He established a relationship with His people in a covenant, declaring himself their God and the people His own. Nothing the Israelites did brought on this great and gracious love: it was all God's will, His choosing, His initiative. Consider this:

The LORD did not choose you and lavish his love on you because you were larger or greater than other nations, for you were the smallest of all nations! It was simply because the LORD loves you, and because he was keeping the oath he had sworn to your ancestors.

DEUTERONOMY 7:7-8 NLT

Because of who you are—a godly parent—you love your children. There's nothing they did or didn't do to earn your love. The very fact that they are your children makes them the recipients of your unconditional love. No child could fully understand the reason for Mommy's or Daddy's love, but you can make sure all of your children know without a doubt that you do love them. You love them simply because they belong to you—the same reason your heavenly Father loves you.

God so loved the world that he gave his one and only Son, that whoever believes in him shall not perish but have eternal life.

JOHN 3:16

In spite of our sin, God loves us. We behave in ways that

offend and anger God, yet God continues to love. Though the children of Israel repeatedly turned away from Him, God kept His loving promise to send a Messiah. God in Jesus Christ confirmed God's love for the world. By His life, death, and resurrection, Jesus says: "I love you." Just as God's love for you transcends anything you might do or say to offend Him, your love for your children goes beyond their behavior and attitude. And because of your love for them, their bad behavior and poor attitude bring you displeasure—after all, if you didn't love them, you wouldn't care! Correction, therefore, signals not a lack of love, but an abundance of love.

**My son, do not make light of the Lord's discipline,
and do not lose heart when he rebukes you,
because the Lord disciplines those he loves,
and he punishes everyone he accepts as a son.**

HEBREWS 12:5-6

In spite of the sins they may commit, you love your children. You demonstrate your love by guiding them with consistent, fair, and firm discipline. Look to the way the Lord guides you. In His Word, He clearly shows you His Commandments and instructs you concerning how He wants you to behave. Knowing you can never live up to His expectations—perfection—God laid out a plan for you. He gave you the gift of His Spirit so you can recognize your sin, repent of it, and obtain forgiveness by grace through faith in Jesus Christ. His Spirit lives and works in you so you can turn from your errors and grow in holiness. The writer of Hebrews put it this way:

**No discipline is enjoyable while it is happening—it is painful!
But afterward there will be a quiet harvest of right living for
those who are trained in this way.**

HEBREWS 12:11 NLT

What an unmistakable sign of God's great love!

As a parent, be sure your children have a clear understanding of your expectations. Remind them. Model for them the behavior you want them to emulate. Be the kind of person you want them to be. But children often fail to measure up to expectations. Why? For as many reasons as we adults fail to measure up to God's perfection. We're weak. We're willful. We're spiritually immature. In other words, we sin. And so do children. Paul speaks for all of us when he laments in Romans:

> **When I want to do good, I don't.**
> **And when I try not to do wrong, I do it anyway.**
>
> **ROMANS 7:19 NLT**

Just as you depend on God to keep you close to Him and His will and desires for your life, your children depend on you to keep them physically, morally, and spiritually safe. Sometimes, you need to correct them by imposing appropriate penalties as the consequence of poor behavior. It's a sign and a proof of your continuous and unconditional love for them.

In doing so, however, don't forget what God does for you. You've experienced the consequences of sin, and you've repented. You have God's forgiveness and the assurance of His love for you. Do the same for your children. Teach them what's right, but forgive them when they do what's wrong. Allow them to experience the temporal consequences of their sinful actions, but assure them of your continuing and unconditional love.

> **"Though the mountains be shaken and the hills be removed,**
> **yet my unfailing love for you will not be shaken nor my**
> **covenant of peace be removed," says the LORD, who has compassion on you.**
>
> **ISAIAH 54:10**

Forever, God loves His children. He promises you His

unchanged and unchanging love every day of your earthly life—and for eternity. You can depend on God's love no matter where you are, in what state of health you're in, whether you're rich or poor, successful in the eyes of others, or ignored by an indifferent world. You need never ask, "God, do you love me?" It's a no-brainer. "No matter what happens," He tells His children, "I love you."

Forever, you'll love your children. As they grow up, they'll learn they can depend on you. They'll see the many ways you show your love, from the sticky-note message you put in their backpack to the constant and attentive care you give them when they're sick. Perhaps not until they're parents themselves will they realize the sacrifices love makes, the distance love goes, the joy love brings—but you know. When you say, "I love you," your heart adds, "forever."

Walk the Talk
Don't Just Preach It—Live It

A recent survey asked teens to name the person they looked up to as a role model. You might suppose they cited singers, celebrities, and sports stars. The majority, however, didn't. They named Mom. They named Dad. Your child looks up to you.

Daily, your children absorb what you do, say, and don't say. They know if you grumble about Grandma around the kitchen table but admonish them to treat her with respect. They see the gap between your lecture on honesty and your approval of creative IRS deductions. They figure your good intention to take the family to church every Sunday is just that—a good intention—if you sleep in most Sundays. Your warnings about the dangers of alcohol will go unheeded if your kids notice you can't have a good time without a glass in your hand.

> *Daily, your children absorb what you do, say, and don't say.*

**So take a new grip with your tired hands and
stand firm on your shaky legs.
Mark out a straight path for your feet.
Then those who follow you, though they are weak and lame,
will not stumble and fall but will become strong.**
HEBREWS 12:12-13 NLT

Give your life and your lifestyle a thorough examination. Do you demonstrate the traits you want your children to acquire? Do you say and do things you're proud to pass on to the next generation? Because whether you like it or not, that's what happens. "Do as I say, not as I do" fails in the face of what actually happens. Kids do what they see done.

The point of your examination is not to make you into a plastic saint, but to open your eyes. The Holy Spirit, present in your heart, constantly works to bring your thoughts, words, and actions in line with God's commandments. But not until heaven will you cease being a work in progress. Paul says:

**I advise you to live according to your new life
in the Holy Spirit. Then you won't be doing what your sinful
nature craves. The old sinful nature loves to do evil, which is
just opposite from what the Holy Spirit wants. And the Spirit
gives us desires that are opposite from what the sinful nature
desires. These two forces are constantly fighting each other,
and your choices are never free from this conflict.**
GALATIANS 5:16-17 NLT

Your children observe how you handle the conflict. They see when you lose a battle—when you sin. Do you admit it or deny it? Do you accept responsibility or blame others? Do you take it seriously or explain it away? If you find your child unable to come to terms with his or her own actions, review how you're handling similar situations. Chances are you'll see a pattern in your own behavior reflected in the behavior of your child. Now you know where change needs to start! Our Lord directs:

> **First get rid of the log from your own eye;**
> **then perhaps you will see well enough to deal with the**
> **speck in your friend's eye.**
>
> **MATTHEW 7:5 NLT**

As a teaching tool, sin ranks as one of the best. When your children observe you doing something wrong, they're likely to come away unsettled, perhaps even frightened. The one they think does everything right does wrong after all. If you try to hide that fact, you will fail. Besides the knowledge of your wrongdoing, your children will also note your hypocrisy. Instead, consider these steps:

1. **Explain the situation with as much detail as your child can understand and is appropriate.** If possible, relate to similar experiences your child might have had.

2. **Take responsibility for what you said or did.** Don't be afraid to admit, "I wish I hadn't done that," or "I should never have said such a thing." Own up to the fact that you hurt someone, caused embarrassment, or feel ashamed.

3. **Talk about the importance of repentance and forgiveness.** State that you know God has forgiven you, because He says so in His Word, and explain, "When we say we're sorry and mean it, Jesus forgives us."

4. **If applicable, say what you plan to do to rectify the wrong.** This

gives your child a practical example of what can and should be done: write a note of apology, pay for damaged property, confess to having told a lie. When your child faces a similar situation, you've made the godly way easier with your example.

5. **Point out that sincere repentance means we resolve, with the help of the Holy Spirit, to do better next time.** Follow through on your intention.

You stand in one of the most sacred positions in God's kingdom on earth as spiritual mentor, guidance counselor, role model to one—or more—of God's little ones. Day to day, you might see more of the challenge than change, more of the frustration than the fruition. But growth, shaping, and development are happening because of God's work through you. And in her eyes—in his eyes—you're a hero already.

The Fun Factor
Having Fun With Your Children

It's been said that Christians have every reason to be happy. How true! From God the Father, we've received the breath of life, material blessings, and all creation. From God the Son, we have forgiveness of sins, assurance of His presence, and the certain promise of life everlasting. From God the Holy Spirit, we're kept in the faith and sanctified—made holy—to better serve God and those around us. The psalmist rightly exclaims:

Let all those rejoice who put their trust in You; let them ever shout for joy, because You defend them; let those also who love Your name be joyful in You.

PSALM 5:11 NKJV

31

Joy in the Lord begins in the heart that trusts in the Lord. Enabled by the Holy Spirit, believers put aside anxiety, fear, and despair and grow in contentment, courage, and confidence. You work diligently for the support of your family, at the same time secure in God's ability and willingness to provide. You face directly the challenges confronting you and those you love because you know Almighty God stands right alongside you. You rest peacefully, "casting all your care upon Him, for He cares for you" (1 Peter 5:7 NKJV). In other words, you can have fun!

Doing wrong is fun for a fool,
while wise conduct is a pleasure
to the wise.
PROVERBS 10:23 NLT

The world has taken over, redefined, and warped many of the God-given pleasures of life. What's so often called entertainment consists of little but lewd diversions that lead to nothing but an appetite for more vulgar displays. Even the word "party" in certain contexts more than suggests alcohol abuse and the use of illegal drugs. As a Christian parent, you need to provide a strong, active, and godly definition of fun.

Your young children depend on you to provide stories, movies, and social opportunities appropriate for their ages and conducive to their intellectual and spiritual development. Later, when they begin choosing for themselves, they will need your guidance and oversight until they can consistently make good choices. They will ask why they can't see a film or watch a TV program "everyone else" finds highly entertaining. They will want to own or download questionable computer games their friends recommend. You need to know why not, and you will know if you're solidly grounded in God's Word. Even in the area of pleasure, godly parents seek godly advice.

You define godly fun most convincingly by having godly fun

yourself. Don't go to questionable movies and don't let your kids hear vulgar dialogue coming from the TV after they've gone to bed. Select clean entertainment for yourself and have fun in wholesome, healthy ways.

> Hang around doggies and kids; they know how to play.
> -Geoffrey Godbey

What's more, have fun every day. Cultivate a cheerful attitude, no matter what you're doing. Smile. "From sour-faced saints," remarked Teresa of Avila, "good Lord, deliver us."

> **If they [believers] obey and serve him,**
> **they will spend the rest of their days**
> **in prosperity and their years**
> **in contentment.**
>
> Job 36:11

Provide balance in your everyday routine by setting aside time to do enjoyable, relaxing things together. This can be as simple as sitting down with your children to read a story or going outside to see what's blooming in the garden. It can also consist of going to church dinners and picnics, meeting with other Christian families for outings, and planning service projects together.

Lean toward activities everyone can get involved in to some extent. In so doing, you'll be teaching older children to appreciate the contributions of younger children, as well as allowing bonds to form between them—the stuff of treasured memories in the future.

Granted, there will be times work and other responsibilities need to come first. The lesson of delayed gratification for the sake of serving others in business, or in the family, church, or community will work to your children's advantage. But if they consistently see a pattern of family time fit in only "when there's time," they'll soon seek their pleasures elsewhere.

33

**Better a little with righteousness than
much gain with injustice.**

PROVERBS 16:8

Much of the world's entertainment puts a big dent in the pocketbook of the average family. If you find too much of your budget devoted to recreational activities, it might be time to review your spending habits and prioritize your needs and wants. Debt is no fun! You can provide a much more stable, happy household if it's free of money worries than you can if it's stocked with the latest toys and photo albums of exotic vacations.

In addition, you'll be demonstrating through example that you don't need to overspend, overconsume, and overdo to have a good time.

Enriching activities are part of God's good creation. They begin with the joy of being together and having the blessing of each other's company. They include discovery—your own backyard is a good place to start—as well as giggles, silliness, and laughter. They end with a feeling of wholesome pleasure and continue to live in the fond memories shared by a godly family. Truly, fun is a gift of God!

**Whether you eat or drink or whatever you do,
do it all for the glory of God.**

1 CORINTHIANS 10:31

The Art of Showing Interest
Cultivating Your Children's Interests

> **God saw all that he had made,**
> **and it was very good.**
>
> **GENESIS 1:31**

A symphony violinist, asked how she happened to take up the violin as a child, claimed no earth-shattering revelation. No one tapped her at two years old as a musical prodigy. Rather, she happened to live in the same neighborhood as a little girl who took violin lessons. She thought this little girl looked "pretty cool" walking with her violin case from the bus stop to her home. Thus, a humble beginning to what became a rich and fulfilling career for the symphony violinist!

Oftentimes, our interests grow and develop as we observe others doing "pretty cool" things. How long has it been since you've taken up a new hobby, learned a new skill, shared a new interest with someone else? Under the multiple responsibilities of raising a family, you might consider yourself too busy—or too old—to take on new projects. Or you might think raising children poses enough new discoveries to last a lifetime! Possibly true—but the key to getting your children to cultivate varied interests is to get interested yourself.

> When you're young, the silliest notions seem the greatest achievements.
> -Pearl Bailey

Take a moment to step into your children's shoes. Do they see you excited to take on projects and willing to try new things? Do they hear you praise the efforts and enthusiasm of others, even though they're not the "stars" of the show? Will they remember you as someone who opened doors—or someone who closed them?

He is the God who made the world
and everything in it.

ACTS 17:24 NLT

Open doors for yourself. Let your kids see how rewarding it is to develop special skills, hobbies, specialties, and talents. Then, be a door opener for them.

★ When a subject engages your child, take time to explore it together. Don't rush to judgment as to whether your child has the talent, possesses the ability, will stick with it. If your child shows continued interest, you may need to bring up any limitations, such as physical, financial, or time, and work to resolve the issues.

★ A child's enthusiasm for something is often short-lived. Progress slowly in following up with his or her expressed interests to gauge whether or not the interest has life beyond a passing fancy. If your child takes on too many projects at once, he risks finding satisfaction in none. If your child constantly starts something new and then quits after a short time, she may begin to consider herself good at nothing.

★ Provide encouragement when your child's desire to participate flags. No matter how talented your child may be, or how earnestly he or she wants to pursue an interest, there are bound to be times of weariness, frustration, and discouragement. Explain that these feelings are normal and generally temporary. Even the zealous apostle Paul needed to give himself a pep talk from time to time. "I press on toward the goal to win the prize for which God has called me heavenward in Christ Jesus," he wrote in Philippians 3:14.

★ Well-chosen activities and hobbies can lead to a lifetime of pleasure—or not. While the decision to quit the team, abandon the stamp collection, or discontinue piano lessons should not be taken lightly, there can come the time when your child needs to move on to something else. Only you can help determine the best course of action when one of your children wants to give up.

Well-chosen activities and hobbies can lead to a lifetime of pleasure.

★ Provide an interest-rich environment for your children. As appropriate to their ages and the accessibility of various venues, frequently take them to the library, on nature walks, to children's plays, musicals, and other programs. Explain what's happening when you watch sports together, attend Little League games, go to major sports events. Plan recreational/educational day trips and vacations.

★ Make it possible for your children to get involved in extracurricular activities at school, and encourage participation.

★ Take every opportunity to remind your children that gifts and talents are given by God and are to be used for His purposes. You will be the one to lift their vision higher than the development of talent to a plane of eternal opportunities and rewards. Give your children a sense that they should be asking how they can use their gifts for God's glory. And remember, your greatest influence comes from your children seeing you acknowledge God as the Source of your talents and the One who is showing you how to use those talents to the fullest for His purposes.

**I was glad when they said unto me,
Let us go into the house of the Lord.**

Psalm 122:1 KJV

Igniting and maintaining your children's interest in church ranks as your highest responsibility. The evening before church services, remind your young children where the family will be going the next day. In terms they can understand, talk about why you're going, what you're going to do, and what you expect their behavior to be. End with a few words about how much you're looking forward to being in God's house and with His people.

Interest in church often wanes as children hit the teen years. It's vitally important to help them maintain interest by supporting and assisting in your church's youth ministry. If you detect gaps in programs designed for youth, see what you and other parents of teens can do.

**Oh, how great is Your goodness,
which You have laid up for those who fear You,
which You have prepared for those who trust in You in the
presence of the sons of men!**

PSALM 31:19 NKJV

You never know where your child's interests will lead. Today, their interests lead them to explore the world, develop their talents, and find the satisfaction of doing something worthwhile, productive, and pleasurable. Tomorrow, their interests may become a career, a special expertise, a fulfilling activity, a lifelong passion. Always, your children will remember you as the one who believed in them enough to let them try new, different, fun, and creative things.

Stepping Up to the Plate
Taking Responsibility for Your Children's Spiritual Growth

**Children are a gift from the LORD;
they are a reward from him.**

PSALM 127:3 NLT

What do you want your children to remember about you? If you are bringing them up in the Christian faith, you're leaving them a legacy that will last from now through eternity. You're the one who took them to church, heard their bedtime prayers, and brought them up in the way of the Lord. Blessed memories, indeed! And a godly example as they raise their own children.

Timothy, the apostle Paul's protégé and companion in ministry, grew up in a godly family. Writing to Timothy from prison in Rome, Paul encouraged the young pastor in Ephesus to remain zealous in the Lord's work. "I know that you sincerely trust the Lord," Paul wrote in 2 Timothy 1:5 (NLT), "for you have the faith of your mother, Eunice, and your grandmother, Lois." Because of Timothy's early training and continued love for the Lord, he became a faithful and effective leader in the early Christian church.

Remember the Sabbath day, to keep it holy.
EXODUS 20:8 NKJV

Spiritual training starts early—in infancy, in fact. Let your baby hear and absorb the sounds, songs, and cadences of God's people at worship. Let him be present for the whisperings of the Holy Spirit in his heart. Let her breathe in the fragrance of prayer and praise being lifted up to God in His sanctuary. Let one of your child's very first memories be the blessing of sitting in the house of God with you.

Your faithful and regular church attendance establishes the priority that worship and spiritual growth are afforded in your household. Never will your young child ask "if we're going to church" on the Lord's Day. If it's the Lord's Day, we're going to church. Begin your child's spiritual training on the solid ground of faithful, active worship.

*Begin your child's spiritual training
on the solid ground of faithful,
active worship.*

You can help your young children pay attention in church by asking them about what they learned in Sunday school or the children's sermon. Reinforce points and add others they may have missed. Use what your children say as a stepping-stone to a longer conversation, thus letting them know their attention will be rewarded with your time and attention.

Teens may resist your efforts to get them to church, claiming worship lacks interest or relevance. You may need to exercise your authority as the parent, enforcing the rule that in your house, church attendance is mandatory. Nonetheless, be sure your worship community includes a vibrant youth ministry. If it doesn't, see what you can do to make it happen. Teens have questions, and you want to make sure yours have access to Christ-centered answers.

Spiritual training, however, doesn't end at the church door. It's encouraged, nurtured, and fortified in the home. When you consider how many hours you spend in church versus the hours you have at home with your children, you quickly realize who's your children's primary spiritual leader—you are.

> **You fathers—if your children ask for a fish,
> do you give them a snake instead?
> Or if they ask for an egg,
> do you give them a scorpion?
> Of course not!**
>
> LUKE 11:11-12 NLT

Offering your children a sound spiritual diet is like seeing to a nutritious physical diet: You need to prepare and serve healthy meals. No fast-food substitutes will do!

★ "Oh, give thanks to the LORD, for He is good!" (Psalm 118:1 NKJV). Establish the tradition of praying before and after meals. Not only will you be instilling a God-honoring practice but also effectively counteracting the unhealthy trend to bypass family sit-down meals for an eat-on-the-go diet.

★ "Keep on praying" (1 Thessalonians 5:17 NLT). Teach young children simple bedtime prayers. Encourage them to remember their parents, grandparents, and other important people in their prayers. This bedtime ritual reminds children of God's presence, strengthens the bonds of family love, and surrounds them with God's peace throughout the night.

41

★ "My mouth will speak words of wisdom; the utterance from my heart will give understanding" (Psalm 49:3). Discuss issues from a biblical perspective. As appropriate for your children's ages, talk about hot topics and controversial issues. Let your children know they can bring up anything and you will respond with truthful, Bible-centered, God-honoring dialogue.

★ "All Scripture is inspired by God and is useful to teach us what is true and to make us realize what is wrong in our lives. It straightens us out and teaches us to do what is right" (2 Timothy 3:16 NLT). Immerse yourself in Scripture, and put God's Word in the hands of your children at an early age. (Bibles for children and teens are available in Christian bookstores or can be ordered online from Christian publishers.) For yourself, seek out adult Bible study opportunities and read spiritual books. The more you know, the more you grow, and the more you can pass on to your children.

★ "I will meditate on Your precepts, and contemplate Your ways" (Psalm 119:15 NKJV). Be sure everyone in your household has a place to go for private meditation and prayer, and that there's a quiet time during the day or evening conducive to contemplation. If possible, set up a lamp, chair, and small bookcase with a Bible and spiritual books so anyone in need of a little time out with God can find a quiet place.

**So we, being many, are one body in Christ,
and individually members of one another.**

ROMANS 12:5 NKJV

You have a big job, but you're not alone. Cultivate the friendship of other godly parents. Share tips, frustrations, challenges, and joys. Take full advantage of the blessing God has given you in caring relatives, pastors, friends, and fellow parishioners. But no matter who's with you or who's against you, remember that you—and your children—belong to God. Remain faithful.

As for me and my household, we will serve the LORD.

JOSHUA 24:15

Shaping the Will
Discipline—the How, What, When, Where, and Why

**Train up a child in the way he should go:
and when he is old, he will not depart from it.**

PROVERBS 22:6 KJV

Parents don many hats, but disciplinarian often ranks as the one they would rather not wear. We don't want to play the "heavy," the one who lays down the law and metes out punishment. We don't enjoy causing kids to cry, get angry, receive time-outs, or lose privileges. Yet, God has given parents the authority to train their children in the way they should go. And with that authority comes the responsibility to keep them going in the right direction.

For the Christian parent, discipline is not an option. It's a God-given duty.

> **The Spirit himself testifies with our spirit
> that we are God's children.**
>
> **ROMANS 8:16**

Our heavenly Father did not create us, then leave us to our own devices. In His mercy, He didn't say, "Okay—now you go do whatever seems best to you." If He had, imagine what a mess we'd find ourselves in! We'd need to decipher for ourselves the meaning of our own existence. By a process of trial and error, we'd have to figure out what's harmful to us and what's beneficial. And if we ever got around to thinking about God, we'd have no idea whether or not He loves us, whether or not we're pleasing Him.

Our God loves His children much more than that. In His compassion for our human frailty, He created us, then said:

> **It is the LORD your God you must follow,
> and him you must revere.
> Keep his commands and obey him;
> serve him and hold fast to him.**
>
> **DEUTERONOMY 13:4**

God's Law is the standard by which we compare our thoughts, words, and actions. The path from spiritual immaturity to maturity is lined with lessons, and many of them involve the unhappy consequences of ill-chosen behavior. And these are the lessons we tend to remember quite well. Were there no particular consequences for doing wrong, we'd have little reason or incentive to do right.

Your children need—and want—your clearly defined rules,

guidance, and expectations. To give your words substance, just punishment must follow broken rules, ignored guidance, and willfully unmet expectations. If your children realize nothing happens if they choose to disobey you, they'll stop obeying you, or even listening to you. God doesn't work that way, and neither should you. Discipline means clearly defining your rules and enforcing them.

> **Don't make your children angry by the way you treat them. Rather, bring them up with the discipline and instruction approved by the Lord.**
> **EPHESIANS 6:4 NLT**

God gave us His Law—but not just His Law. If He had done so, we would be engaged in a futile attempt to attain perfection and exist in perpetual fear of punishment. God balances His Law with His Gospel. We're incapable of God's holiness—His perfection—so He promised a Savior whose righteousness is ours by God's grace through faith in Jesus. In Jesus, we have access to full forgiveness for the sins and offenses we commit against God and our neighbor.

Discipline and instruction approved by the Lord offers children both Law and Gospel. Define your rules, enforce your rules—and accept repentance, offer forgiveness. That doesn't mean no punishment, but it does mean punishment appropriate to the infraction, child's age, attitude, and particular circumstances.

Discipline and instruction approved by the Lord offer children both Law and Gospel.

Harsh, humiliating, insensitive discipline does nothing to further your child's respect for rules. It only serves to build up anger and resentment. The Lord consistently disciplines you with kindness. Despite anything you may have done or ever will do against Him and His Commandments, you have His forgiveness in Jesus Christ. Express your deepest gratitude to your Father in heaven by disciplining your child with and in the kindness of Christ. Use discipline as just one more way you demonstrate to your child God's love and care. Jesus said:

"Whoever welcomes one of these little children in my name welcomes me; and whoever welcomes me does not welcome me but the one who sent me."

MARK 9:37

While God's Commandments never change, your rules and expectations undergo transformation as children grow older, as circumstances shift, as new challenges arise and others diminish. Consistency rests not necessarily in the outward appearance of your rules and expectations, but in the principle behind them. For you, that principle is God's Word. When your children know where your values come from, they realize the context of your rules and expectations. As they grow older and away from your constant supervision, they will have in your training a biblically firm foundation for self-discipline and self-control.

The father of godly children has cause for joy. What a pleasure it is to have wise children. So give your parents joy! May she who gave you birth be happy.

PROVERBS 23:24-25 NLT

At the time, giving or receiving discipline seems a largely thankless and joyless task. Yet, godly discipline yields rewards both temporal and eternal. While we live on earth and in community with one another, we need rules for the smooth running of society. Parents impress them on their children for their safety and for the safety of others, and so children can grow into productive adults in fulfilling relationships. As we look forward to life everlasting, we need rules to keep us mindful of God's will for our salvation. He impresses His Commandments on His children so we can see where we have sinned and avoid dangers to our spiritual health. God's discipline and the discipline of godly parents is nothing less than an expression of love.

Love your children. Love them enough to discipline them.

Presence vs. Presents
The Importance of Spending Quality Time Together

> **The Lord replied, "My Presence will go with you, and I will give you rest."**
> **EXODUS 33:14**

Your children will remember the value of your presence far longer than the cost of your presents. While most people acknowledge the inability of money to buy the best things in life, many parents use money, even subconsciously, to buy what essentially can't be bought.

Your children will remember the value of your presence far longer than the cost of your presents.

Most parents find a great deal of pleasure in giving gifts to their children. We like to watch their faces light up when they unwrap exactly what they've been asking for. We delight in their glee in trying out their shiny new bicycle or in showing off to their friends the hottest computer game, all presents from Mom and Dad. But their excitement turns hollow when the gifts merely mask what we don't give—the gift of our time.

Parents who use purchased presents to fill a void caused by their withheld presence send false, destructive messages to their children:

★ Gifts relieve guilt.

★ You can buy your way out of your duties and obligations to others.

★ Measure the magnitude of love by the price tag of the gift.

★ Material things are more important than human relationships.

★ If you want to make someone happy, give a gift.

★ If Mom and Dad lavish kids with gifts, parents have a right to say "no" when kids ask for things that call for personal sacrifice—such as time, effort, attention.

God certainly isn't anti-gift. His gift to us in Jesus Christ came because of His love for His children. His precious present to us in Jesus demonstrates God's presence in our lives.

> **"The virgin will be with child and will give birth to a son, and they will call him Immanuel"—which means, "God with us."**
> **MATTHEW 1:23**

In addition, God gave us all creation and daily showers us with those things we need to provide for ourselves and our families. He blesses families by granting them the pleasures of homespun comforts, fantastic extras, world-class luxuries. As God in His goodness blesses you with any number of material gifts, most assuredly He plans for you to share His blessings

47

with your children. But just as our heavenly Father, in His goodness and mercy, measures out your gifts according to His wisdom, you, too, need to exercise godly wisdom in managing the place held by material things in your family.

Take a few minutes to describe the gifts you recently have given your children. Think back to last Christmas, the last birthday party, and any other time during the past year you have given both small and significant gifts to your children. Ask yourself:

★ Could you well afford the presents you selected?

★ Did you buy because you were feeling guilty for not being home, missing last season's ball game, or forgetting about the school play?

★ Is your child becoming less and less enthusiastic about receiving gifts?

★ Does your child quickly tire of the gifts you buy?

If your response to any of these questions gives you pause, you might be inadvertently sending the wrong message about gifts to your children. Under the guise of giving your children "everything they ask for," or "all they could ever need," you might be ignoring what they're really asking for, what they truly need— your time, your attention, your presence.

> **You know the grace of our Lord Jesus Christ, that though he was rich, yet for your sakes he became poor, so that you through his poverty might become rich.**
>
> 2 CORINTHIANS 8:9

When the budget and your values establish the level of gift giving in your family, you're ready to focus on gifts that really matter. The first one, of course, is your time. Parents—most particularly mothers—who work outside the home in addition to raising their children face a daily battle with time. The urgent demands of children and a career simply outnumber the minutes in any given day. If you find yourself in this situation right now, stop and take your most pressing needs to your Lord in prayer.

Your words may sound something like this:

Heavenly Father,
Thank you for always being present in my life and available to me. Like a little child, I come to you now, needing your open arms, your comfort, your strength. I'm torn between what I have to do to support my family and what I want to do to nurture my children. I have failed in many respects, and I beg your forgiveness. Give me the courage I need to make tough, even sacrificial, choices. Help me live in such a way that my family has no doubt about my love, care, and commitment. In Jesus' name I pray.
Amen.

The second gift that really matters is your attention. When you have time with your children, how do you spend it? Too many of us have seen a mother or father yapping on a cell phone while their hapless child sits staring into space. Time with your children counts for little more than supervision (and a baby-sitter could just as easily do that) if a cell phone, TV, magazine, or best friend has your attention.

The third gift—and the most important—is your love. While your gift of love is clearly expressed in the quality of your time and attention, a gift given from the heart can be a cherished reminder of your presence when your presence must be in spirit only. A little note tucked inside her book bag—a card on his night-stand—a funny phone message on her voice mail—a little bouquet of flowers "just because you're you." Give the gift of yourself, and let your kids discover how rich they really are with a treasure they'll remember forever.

> **We pray this in order that you may live a life worthy of the Lord**
> **and may please him in every way: bearing fruit in every good**
> **work, growing in the knowledge of God.**
>
> COLOSSIANS 1:10

The Test of Time
Forming Healthy Boundaries and Healthy Schedules

> **For everything there is a season,**
> **and a time for every matter under heaven.**
>
> ECCLESIASTES 3:1 NRSV

"There's just not enough time!" How often do you hear yourself saying that? Chances are, several times a day if you're the parent of school-age children. Naturally, you want to give them every available opportunity to develop academically, physically, and socially. We know college admissions boards regularly look at a prospective student's record of community service in addition to grades, awards, and special achievements. From an early age, kids follow a tight schedule just to get everything in.

Tight schedules, however, allow little time for kids to be kids. They often lack free, unstructured time to think, draw, write, discover books, or see elephants and dragons in the shapes of the clouds. Are children's overly structured schedules edging out creative spirits and fruitful imaginations? Are we, as a society, placing too much emphasis on objective accomplishment as opposed to spiritual fulfillment? Only you can answer those questions as they relate to your children.

50

Tight schedules allow little time for kids to be kids.

Trust in the LORD with all your heart; do not depend on your own understanding. Seek his will in all you do, and he will direct your paths.

PROVERBS 3:5-6 NLT

The job of keeping a sane schedule falls to you, the parent. And as in the case of so many other aspects of parenting, the first place to start is with yourself. What does your schedule look like? You exhibit your values and your priorities by how, where, and with whom you spend your time.

★ **Worship time**. Does regular and faithful church attendance anchor each week? God, the Creator and Giver of time, has specific instructions on how to use it. Jesus tells us to put our heavenly Father first. He says in Matthew 6:33: "Seek first his kingdom and his righteousness, and all these things will be given to you as well."

★ **Family time**. How important are family meals? Studies have uncovered multiple benefits to the whole family when meals are taken together at least several times a week. Family meals are likely to be more wholesome than single-serving on-the-go food. The act of getting together at a set hour signals to children the primacy of family time. Kitchen table conversations work to build and strengthen family bonds. Many families make a tradition of reserving one evening a week for a special dinner followed by board games or other family activities.

★ **School and work time.** Your children will learn from you how to approach their schoolwork by the way you approach your responsibilities. If you're a workaholic, your children grow resentful of the time you spend at work, and hence work itself. On the other hand, if you sigh, grumble, and moan under the weight of your

51

work, your children will pick up the idea that work is a terrible burden and best avoided. If you do as little as possible, your children will think little effort suffices. "Never lag in zeal and in earnest endeavor; be aglow and burning with the Spirit, serving the Lord" (Romans 12:11 AMP).

★ **Recreation time**. "All work and no play makes Jack a dull boy" (and pretty stressed out, too). We're not robots. We need time to unwind, to follow our own musings, to just relax. For yourself, declare downtime. You'll be a more attentive and mindful parent if you do. Be sure your children have downtime for themselves each day. Many parents set aside quiet time each evening so children can calm down and do something relaxing before getting ready for bed.

Though you set limitations on activities for your children, things will come up to challenge even the most carefully constructed calendar. The requirements of a coach—the needs of a school project—an opportunity to join a special-interest club—all kinds of really fun things to do vie for your children's attention. How you handle them shows your children how to manage time.

Begin by assessing how important the new activity is to your child. Ask why your child wants to participate and what he or she expects to get out of it. Discern passing enthusiasm from serious interest.

Then, if the activity proves worthwhile, help your child determine how he or she will find time to pursue it. What will have to be given up? Is the child okay with the trade-off? Do you approve?

Sometimes certain activities can be pursued at a later, more convenient, time. Tell your child why you think he or she should wait and when the activity can be more favorably scheduled. Unless a real reason intervenes, follow through on the plan you've shared with your child.

Time is God's gift to you. He intends for you to neither

squander it in inattentive, aimless pastimes, nor to squash it underfoot with frenetic activity. Rather, He has blessed you with time and given you His directives for the right use of time so you and your children can have the time of your lives.

The Humble Heart
Saying "I'm Sorry"

**[God] guides the humble in what is right
and teaches them his way.**

PSALM 25:9

As the English poet Alexander Pope observed, "To err is human, to forgive divine." How true! We make mistakes. We sin, even willfully. Yet we find it hard to admit our faults—to say, "I'm sorry." A quick cover-up, clever shifting of the blame, or outright denial comes easier than a simple and sincere apology, especially where kids are concerned. They think you're always right—you know everything—you're perfect. Why change their opinion by admitting you're wrong? Because, of course, small impressionable children very quickly become big skeptical children.

If from a young age, they have heard you admit to mistakes and ask forgiveness—if "I'm sorry" comes naturally off your lips—they will develop a balanced idea of what it's like to be human. Your children know full well they make mistakes—after all, you're the one who points them out. From your example, they learn what to do about them.

53

**If we claim to be without sin,
we deceive ourselves and the truth is not in us.**

1 JOHN 1:8

Ideals and self-expectations aside, there's no such thing as the "perfect parent." You're going to say things you wish you hadn't, even potentially damaging things. You're going to take actions that prove to have been the wrong ones. Somewhere along the line, you're going to unintentionally fail your child in some way. Yes, you're a loving, caring, godly parent. But you're also human.

Sin infects and affects each of us and our relationships. Selfishness raises its ugly head in the hearts of even the most self-sacrificing parents. The sparks of anger touch off feelings that shame us, and the pressure of our responsibilities gives way to flawed thinking and poor judgment.

*People who fly into a rage always
make a bad landing!*

For you—a believing Christian—these things serve to bring you to the foot of the cross of your Savior. He died so you can go to Him and unload the burden of your sins. He rose from the dead so you can exchange your guilt for His righteousness. Why not spend a few minutes right now telling your Lord about the last time you lost your temper—became impatient—said something hurtful? Then trust in His forgiveness. Reach out to Him for strength.

**If we confess our sins, he is faithful and just and
will forgive us our sins and purify us from
all unrighteousness.**

1 JOHN 1:9

When a mistake on your part affects your child, apologize in a simple and age-appropriate way. Your children need to hear you admit, "I was wrong, and I'm sorry." Take responsibility for your actions with words such as, "Mommy is tired, and that's why she yelled at you," or "Yes, I forgot to remind you to take your project to school today. Next time, we'll put a note next to your backpack, okay?" For older children, you may want to elaborate so they can understand some of the forces outside themselves at work in your life, and perhaps enlist their help in alleviating or resolving the problem.

Apologies from parent to child and from child to parent promote honest communication. If you are direct about your mistakes, your children will realize it's okay to fess up in clear, candid terms. Your children, knowing you can confront your own mistakes, will feel comfortable coming to you if you have inadvertently hurt them. Apologies defuse pent-up anger and harbored bitterness.

> Lord, where we are wrong, make us willing to change; where we are right, make us easy to live with!
>
> -Rev. Peter Marshall

Parents, of course, want to appear strong. And in God's economy, what the world calls weak—humility—God approves as strength. Perhaps that's why He makes such a big deal about our coming to Him in repentance! We need to learn how from our heavenly Father. We need the Spirit-induced practice of saying "I'm sorry" as we grow in awareness of our many sins. And we need to share the God-given strength of our humility with our children.

Your godly example reflects Christ's example. Jesus says in Matthew 11:29, "Take my yoke upon you and learn from me, for I am gentle and humble in heart, and you will find rest for your souls." His "yoke" is the obligation of a Christlike lifestyle, which includes humbly asking for and receiving forgiveness from Him and from those we have offended. You'll never learn false pride from Jesus, King of Kings, the willing and selfless Servant of all. In the words of sincere apology, there is the strength of

Almighty God and the peace of an untroubled conscience.

The gracious forgiveness Christ holds out to us gives us a template for how we accept the apologies of others. When your children come to you with an apology—thank them. Assure them of your continued love and praise them for their honesty. Let them know it isn't easy to come forward and admit it when we've done something wrong. While an apology won't deflect certain consequences of our actions (for example, unkind words cannot be unsaid), it's important to tell people we're sorry when we've done something to hurt them.

[Jesus said,] "Whoever welcomes this little child in my name welcomes me; and whoever welcomes me welcomes the one who sent me. For he who is least among you all —he is the greatest."

LUKE 9:48

When you show your children the gracious humility of a simple and sincere apology, you welcome them into the spiritual lifestyle. You are modeling your attitude toward Christ, your ability and willingness to bend your knee—and in so doing, you gain a stature no other posture confers. God calls it "the greatest." And don't be too surprised if your children start using those words too!

Ready, Set, Go for It!
Commissioned as a Godly Parent

As you can see, raising godly children is inextricably linked to becoming a godly parent. With so much of eternal importance hanging in the balance, you might be asking how you can possibly pull it off. This is no Sunday-morning, best-behavior performance. Being a godly parent means practicing godliness every minute of every day. After all, your kids live with you—not much escapes their eagle eyes.

Before you faint at the daunting task before you, however, think about this. God does not expect you to walk in godliness on your own. He has promised to be with you, to guide you with insight and encouragement, and nudge you when you aren't measuring up. By His grace, He has promised to endue your efforts with power. He won't abandon you without hope and without resources. You can count on Him! Absolutely—without reservation.

> *God does not expect you to walk in godliness on your own.*

So tackle your appointed assignment with gusto whether you have one child or twenty—God is with you, on your side, always watching, always coming to your rescue, always making His wisdom and mighty resources available to you.

Now that you've prepared yourself, it's time to focus directly on your children. Take a deep breath, whisper a prayer—here we go!

Hand in Hand, a Child and I

Dear Lord, I do not ask that Thou shouldst give me
some high work of Thine,

Some noble calling or some wondrous task;

Give me a little hand to hold in mine;

Give me a child to point the way

Over the strange sweet path that leads to Thee;

Give me a little voice to teach to pray;

Give me two shining eyes Thy face to see.

The only crown I ask, dear Lord, to wear is this—

That I may teach a little child.

I do not ask that I should stand among the wise,
the worthy, or the great:

I only ask that softly, hand in hand,

A child and I may enter at Thy gate.

Author Unknown

Secrets for Growing Godly Kids

**Point your kids in the right direction—
when they're old they won't be lost.**

PROVERBS 22:6 MSG

Knowing God
Helping Your Kids Develop a Loving, Personal Relationship with Their Creator

A song made popular in the early 1950s titled "To Know You Is to Love You," inadvertently states a profound spiritual truth when applied to God: To know Him is to love Him. And loving God is, after all, the ultimate goal of every parent for his or her child.

Loving God is the ultimate goal of every parent for his or her child.

But how do you teach your children to know God when they cannot see God?

The story goes that one little boy inclined his face toward the air vents in his bedroom every night when he knelt to pray. His mother questioned him about this habit: "Son, why do you pray toward the air vents?"

"Because you said He hears my prayers, Mom. That means He's within earshot; and since I've looked everywhere else, I figure He must be hiding up there."

The first obstacle in teaching children about God is helping them to understand His invisible nature. You teach them to believe in a God they cannot see, pray to a God they cannot see, and worship a God that never shows His face at church. It makes it difficult for children to grasp how real, how powerful, and how present He is.

Knowing God in Nature. Though your children cannot see God, they can see evidence of Him everywhere if you'll teach them to interpret what they are seeing. The most obvious opportunities are in the great outdoors. Nature provides a panorama of proof:

★ the detail and design in a flower, tree, or leaf

★ the personality in a puppy

★ the organization among ants

★ the formation of geese as they fly

★ the engineering genius of a beaver

★ the amazing architecture of a honeycomb

★ the force and energy of fire

★ the power and serenity of water

★ the root structure of plants

★ the aerodynamics of an eagle in flight

One field trip out-of-doors can turn into a day of discovery about the God who created the world—His flair for design, His appreciation of variety, His incredible knowledge, His artistic bent, His tenderness, and His sense of humor. God's personality is painted on the canvas of creation with amazing clarity.

Knowing God in the Nature of Man. Another way to learn about God is to observe the nature of man. Mankind was created in His image. Since God is good, then that which is noblest, purest, and best within men and women represents the image of God. The characteristics we recognize as love, generosity, mercy, kindness, tenderness, strength, courage, sacrifice are attributes belonging to the Almighty. These—the traits that draw us to people—are the very things about God that draw us to Him as well.

Teach your children to read people in much the same way they would read a book.

1. **Read what is there in black and white**—the overt messages that people intend: their words and actions.

2. **Read what is between the lines**—the less obvious signals: their body language, facial expressions, tone of voice, mannerisms, and gestures.

3. **There are the notes that you make in their margins**—the space in people's lives where you find their recurring habits, lifestyles, choice of friends, values, talents, preferences, and integrity.

It is inspiring to identify traits and habits in people that the Scriptures identify in God. Your children can find evidence of their Creator in the creature and learn a valuable skill in relating to people at the same time.

The apostle Peter said, "You love him even though you have never seen him. Though you do not see him, you trust him; and even now you are happy with a glorious, inexpressible joy. Your reward for trusting him will be the salvation of your souls" (1 Peter 1:8-9 NLT).

It is possible to love God without ever seeing Him; however, there is one way your child can actually see Him.

Knowing God in the Nature of Jesus. The most critical evidence God ever presented as an argument for His own existence was Jesus. "The Son is the radiance of God's glory and the exact representation of his being" (Hebrews 1:3).

A little girl asked her daddy, "Does God have a face?"

Her daddy replied, "Yes, as a matter of fact, He does."

"Can I see it?" she pressed.

"Sure," he answered.

"Where?" she insisted.

"Do you remember when we read in the Bible about the little girl Jesus healed?"

"Yes, I do!" she exclaimed, proud of her Bible knowledge.

"How do you think He looked when He performed that miracle?"

She softened her countenance and presented her daddy with a tender face.

"That's right," he said. "And when Jesus called Peter out of the boat to walk on that stormy sea in the middle of the night, how do you think Jesus looked?"

She changed her features to that of anticipation and excitement.

"That's right!" he applauded. "And what about when Jesus called Lazarus out of the tomb. What do you think Jesus looked like then?"

She assumed a look of authority—decisive and determined.

"Very good!" he announced.

"How about when He held the babies and blessed them?"

She smiled lovingly and winked.

"Yes!" he shouted. "And what about when with His dying breath Jesus said, 'Father, forgive them. They don't know what they are doing'?"

The little girl looked sad, but hopeful.

"You've got it," the father exclaimed. "Jesus wore the face of God, and you recognized it in every situation."

Jesus said, "And this is the way to have eternal life—to know you, the only true God, and Jesus Christ, the one you sent to earth" (John 17:3 NLT).

Knowing God is a lifetime occupation, and you can teach your children to begin now by looking for evidence of God in the world around them, in the people they encounter, and in the story of Jesus. Your children will then croon the chorus of that old song with the tenor of their lives:

"Yes, yes, to know you . . . is to love, love, love you . . . and I do, yes I do, and I do."

Known by Your Actions
Helping Your Kids Develop Godly Character

The development of godly character—that which leads to godly actions—begins with training the hearts and minds of young people. It has become an issue of tremendous social, political, educational, philosophical, moral, and religious debate. On every front, there are those who vociferously proclaim the pros and cons of one approach as opposed to another. At one extreme, there are those who believe that children should not be directed toward any particular belief system; while at the other, they advocate uniformity in every nuance of thought and action.

What is the answer?

God provides an answer that allows for the incredible diversity of personality, background, abilities, temperament types, intellectual acumen, and giftedness within the ethical boundaries provided by His amazing love. He sets before His people a standard of godliness by which each person may measure him- or herself for the sake of continued development in character, yet with the latitude to exercise one's uniqueness and individuality.

> Be such a man, and live such a life, that if every man were such as you, and every life such as yours, this earth would be God's paradise.
> -Phillip Brooks

Helping your children develop godly character will determine their future in relationships, their spiritual well-being, and their general sense of fulfillment in life. Not to mention that it will make a vast difference in the lives of their fellowman.

In every culture and in every age, core character traits have been singled out and promoted as those that are most desirable in producing respectable men and women. Remarkably, these traits line up with the characteristics produced by the Spirit of God as outlined in Scripture.

64

> **The fruit of the Spirit is love, joy, peace,
> patience, kindness, goodness, faithfulness,
> gentleness and self-control.**
>
> **GALATIANS 5:22-23**

The question is how do you incorporate those characteristics into the fiber of your children's beings? One of the best ways to develop a trait is to develop a habit. In other words, first do, and then you will be. So, for instance, if you were to incorporate loving habits into your family life, your children would become habitually loving people. The same holds true for joyful habits, peaceful habits, and on and on it goes.

One of the best ways to develop a trait is to develop a habit.

How does one develop a habit? Simply by repeating certain behaviors over and over until they become ingrained into one's lifestyle. Take a fresh look at these character traits through the lens of habit and consider ways to turn them into your children's first noble impulses:

★ **The Habit of Love:** An open and wholesome show of affection is a sure path to the development of a loving nature. Have you ever noticed that people who have the habit of hugging are just generally lovable people? Teach your children the appropriate, non-sexual ways to convey an authentic, loving touch to others: a pat on the back, a squeeze of the hand or shoulder, a head rub, a pat on the cheek, or a hug. Emphasize the importance of reaching out to people even when they are undesirable or at their worst. "A man with leprosy came and knelt before him and . . . Jesus reached out his hand and touched the man" (Matthew 8:2-3).

★ **The Habit of Joy:** Small sentiments produce big joys! The habit of saying "Good morning" to others bears a therapeutic benefit both to the sender and the receiver. It is a gracious habit with which to

65

begin the day. For some, mornings are the most difficult part of the day. For others, it is night. One family ends each day by rehearsing the "Best and Worst" events of the day just before prayer time. Each child shares the worst part of his or her day and commits it to the prayers of the rest. Next, they recite the best, ensuring that they end the day with rejoicing and praise. "Through Jesus, therefore, let us continually offer to God a sacrifice of praise— the fruit of lips that confess his name . . . for with such sacrifices God is pleased" (Hebrews 13:15-16).

> Joy is magnified when shared.
> -Tim Hansel

66

★ **The Habit of Peace:** One consistent habit of a peacemaker is taking the initiative in reconciliation. Parents should train their children to make immediate amends for their missteps in relationships, teaching them by example—asking and extending forgiveness themselves—without hesitation. This kind of humility makes a lasting and effective impression of peace upon young hearts. "Do not repay anyone evil for evil. Be careful to do what is right in the eyes of everybody. If it is possible, as far as it depends on you, live at peace with everyone" (Romans 12:17-18).

★ **The Habit of Patience:** One of the most challenging habits to cultivate! Practice a yielding calmness in your character when with your children, especially in the face of adversity, annoyance, and conflict. Assist your children in developing this skill by teaching them to wait quietly and cheerfully—whether waiting for something, someone, or their turn at play. Train your children to hold their tongues and their tempers when their siblings are being obnoxious. And teach them to allow others to go ahead in line, ensuring a long-suffering disposition. "Love is patient. . . . It is not rude, it is not self-seeking, it is not easily angered, it keeps no record of wrongs" (1 Corinthians 13:4-5).

The key to everything is patience!
Don't erupt and don't give up.

★ **The Habit of Kindness:** Get creative! The habits of kindness range from sweet, spontaneous surprises to the hard work of mending broken hearts. Teach your children to write little notes of encouragement to other family members, to fetch someone a glass of water without being asked, to help their siblings when under pressure by tending to the little things yet undone. Teach your children to meet Dad at the door with a hug and a glass of tea, while offering to relieve him of his briefcase. "Therefore, as God's chosen people . . . clothe yourselves with compassion, kindness, humility, gentleness and patience" (Colossians 3:12).

> No one is useless in this world who lightens the burdens of another.
> -Charles Dickens

★ **The Habit of Goodness:** Nurture the habits of honesty, a dependable work ethic, and uprightness of character. Model honesty for your children in uncommon ways—when the status quo commonly opts for little white lies. Be straightforward and direct in all of your communications. Demonstrate routine productivity for your children, accomplishing something worthwhile every day. Resist the temptation to be idle and lazy. "Live as children of light (for the fruit of the light consists in all goodness, righteousness and truth) and find out what pleases the Lord" (Ephesians 5:8-10).

★ **The Habit of Faithfulness:** Set an uncompromising example in your commitments—to your relationship with God, family, church, community, education, your employer, and individuals. A child's capacity for loyalty is directly proportionate to the faithfulness of his or her parents. "Never be lacking in zeal, but keep your spiritual fervor, serving the Lord" (Romans 12:11).

> A lie has speed, but truth has endurance.
> -Edgar J. John

★ **The Habit of Gentleness:** Cultivate tenderness and sensitivity in your children by responding to the lesser heartaches, needs, and desires of people just as readily as you do the big ones. "Blessed are the meek, for they will inherit the earth" (Matthew 5:5).

★ **The Habit of Self-Control:** Model a cheerful and respectful approach to the routine matters of life: health, nutrition, exercise, household chores, hygiene, rest, etc. Teach your children to be selective and moderate in their choices of entertainment, recreation, and friends. "The grace of God . . . has appeared. . . . It teaches us to say 'No' to ungodliness and worldly passions, and to live self-controlled, upright and godly lives" (Titus 2:11-12).

Watch your thoughts;
they become words.
Watch your words;
they become actions.
Watch your actions;
they become habits.
Watch your habits;
they become character.
Watch your character;
it becomes your destiny.

-Frank Outlaw

Good habits and godly character are mutually dependent. One is cause, and the other effect, and vice versa!

The Power and Privilege of Prayer
Teaching Your Kids How to Share Their Hearts With God

Jesus had a passion for prayer. He prayed in public and in private. He prayed deliberately and spontaneously. He prayed intentionally and impulsively. Jesus prayed before making big decisions, and before breaking bread. He prayed over individuals and over cities. He prayed for broken hearts and broken bones. Jesus prayed standing and kneeling. He prayed looking up and lying down. He prayed when He was happy and when He was sad. He enjoyed praying so much that He was known to sneak away while everyone else was sleeping and pray through the night.

But it wasn't really prayer with which Jesus had an obsession. It was the object of His praying—the Almighty Abba. Jesus simply adored His Father. There weren't enough hours in the day to spend in conversation with Him. The fact is, He knew something about prayer that people often miss.

Tucked neatly into the closing sentiments of two short letters, the apostle Paul—mighty man of prayer—reveals five riveting perspectives that can make a profound difference in the prayer life of any believer—especially your child's. He said it this way:

> **Be full of joy in the Lord always. I will say again, be full of joy. . . . Do not worry about anything, but pray and ask God for everything you need, always giving thanks. And God's peace, which is so great we cannot understand it, will keep your hearts and minds in Christ Jesus.**
>
> **PHILIPPIANS 4:4,6-7 NCV**

> **Always be joyful. Pray continually, and give thanks whatever happens. That is what God wants for you in Christ Jesus.**
>
> **1 THESSALONIANS 5:16-18 NCV**

Abbreviate those principles for the sake of learning and you have:

- ★ A joyful anticipation.
- ★ A confident participation.
- ★ A heartfelt conversation.
- ★ A relentless continuation.
- ★ A genuine appreciation.

Consider these perspectives one by one, giving some deliberate thought about how to impress them upon your child's heart and mind:

A Joyful Anticipation. Your youngsters need to know that when they enter the throne room, they are approaching a Father who loves them deeply, who rejoices over them completely, and answers them generously. Teach your children to grasp that their presence brings joy to the Father's heart. Encourage them to see God smiling at the sight of them, to know that they have brightened the Father's face. Once your children have an image of God rejoicing over them, they will find great joy in spending time with Him in prayer.

The LORD your God is with you. He is a hero who saves you. He happily rejoices over you, renews you with his love, and celebrates over you with shouts of joy.

ZEPHANIAH 3:17 GOD'S WORD

A Confident Participation. Children in society have come a long way from the days of their great-grandparents who were told to "speak only when spoken to." In today's culture, adults encourage child-centered conversations and activities. It is a matter of parental prerogative to determine in which social settings children should or should not exercise outspokenness. However, there is one place where your children should be assured that they can speak without reserve—that is the place of prayer. One young mother was astonished to learn how effective she had been in teaching her little boy confidence and confidentiality as he prayed: "Lord, remember I promised to be good if you won't tell Mom what I did; so let's just keep it between you and me."

Let's walk right up to him and get what he is so ready to give. Take the mercy, accept the help.

HEBREWS 4:16 MSG

A Heartfelt Conversation. Children may have difficulty trying to speak from their hearts to a God they cannot touch or see. One dad said, "Honey, you can tell God anything that is on your heart." She stuck out her bottom lip and said, "I don't want to." "Why?" her father probed. "'Cause last night I told Him I was scared and needed someone to talk to, and He didn't talk back." Assure your children that though God doesn't respond audibly, He does respond. Help them discover the answers to their prayers.

I tell you, ask, and God will give to you. Search, and you will find. Knock, and the door will open for you.
LUKE 11:9 NCV

A Relentless Continuation. An old saying goes, "It isn't necessarily that praying changes God's mind, but that praying changes me." Teach your children that the benefit of continual prayer is the integration of one's heart into the will of God. Jesus prayed three times in Gethsemane: at first ... "My way"; at last ... "Thy way." The more your children pray, the more confident and accepting they will be when they finally receive an answer. Their hearts have been fully expressed, and God's response will be thoroughly adequate.

Jesus used this story to teach his followers that they should always pray and never lose hope.... God will always give what is right to his people who cry to him night and day, and he will not be slow to answer them.
LUKE 18:1,7 NCV

A Genuine Appreciation. One of the most profound lessons you can teach your children in prayer is to give heartfelt thanks to God before the prayer is answered. This habit communicates a great deal of trust and reliance upon the Lord. Faith consists in taking hold of the unseen as if it were already in hand. The child who can pray with prevenient gratitude honors

71

God because of his confidence in His faithfulness and love. A teacher approached a child sitting on the curb waiting for his ride. "Do you think your mom has forgotten you?" The little boy looked up at her, beaming, "Forget me? Are you kidding? Without me, my mom wouldn't have anything to remember."

Always give thanks to God the Father for everything, in the name of our Lord Jesus Christ.

EPHESIANS 5:20 NCV

If children learn to pray with this perspective, they will find themselves praying more often, praying more effectively, praying more intimately, and praying in the will of God.

Stealing Away
Helping Your Kids Establish a Daily Quiet Time With God

A habit of daily devotionals is a lifetime struggle for most adults. Is it any wonder that children find the discipline of a daily quiet time so difficult to maintain? After all, the apple doesn't fall far from the tree. Yet, the establishment of such a discipline brings rewards that far outweigh the effort.

Why is it so difficult? Possibly because there aren't enough props in place to support one's attempts at this needful exercise. For example, knowing how difficult it is for a child to get out of bed and into the shower on frosty winter mornings, one mother turns the shower on to warm while she preheats her child's robe in the clothes dryer for smoother transport from the cozy mattress to ceramic tile.

Thousands of years ago, a man named Moses wanted to meet with God in a meaningful way. However, God had said that if any man were to look at Him, he would die. Moses' request for His audience touched the heart of God so deeply that He put props in place that would facilitate Moses' desire. His words to Moses centuries ago still have relevance for your family's meetings with God today. Listen in:

> The LORD said to Moses, "Cut two [more] stone tablets like the first ones. . . . Be ready in the morning. Then come up on Mount Sinai, and stand in my presence on the top of the mountain. No one may come with you or even be seen anywhere on the mountain." . . . So Moses . . . went . . . as the LORD had commanded him. . . . The LORD came down in a cloud and stood there with him and called out his name "the LORD." Then he passed in front of Moses, calling out. . . . Immediately, Moses knelt, bowing with his face touching the ground.
>
> EXODUS 34:1-6, 8 GOD'S WORD

★ **Have dedicated tools** ("Cut two stone tablets . . ."). Make a special trip to the local bookstore and allow each child to purchase a Bible that really appeals to him or her. Such a wide variety of attractive Bibles are available for young people, many with study aids and helps for practical application. Help them find Bibles they can be proud to use and show their friends. Also purchase a special notebook and pen for each child to use during quiet time.

Allow each child to purchase a Bible that really appeals to him or her.

★ **Have a dedicated time** ("Be ready in the morning . . ."). Have an open-minded discussion about what time of day is best for your children's devotional exercise. One dad discovered how to motivate his daughter to keep her commitment—he extended her bedtime by twenty minutes. Help your children set a reasonable expectation concerning how much time their daily devotions should require.

★ **Have a dedicated place** ("Come up on Mount Sinai . . ."). Because human beings are creatures of habit, it is good to have a place set aside and ready for your children's quiet time. You might want to get creative with some storage space—beside the fireplace, in a corner of your kitchen, a desk in the spare bedroom, or even a lofty little spot in your attic. Make certain that your children find the area appealing, comfortable, and secure. Let your youngsters express some creativity by arranging furnishings and organizing their things according to their own preferences.

★ **Dedicate yourself** ("Stand in my presence . . ."). Teach your children the respect with which they should approach the Almighty, but also the confidence with which they can approach Him as His beloved sons and daughters. Train them to honor the Lord with their countenance, tone of voice, and undivided attention. Take the time to explain the wonderful communion they can experience with God when they approach Him with receptive, pure hearts.

Teach your children the respect with which they should approach the Almighty, but also the confidence with which they can approach Him.

★ **Seek some dedicated solitude** ("No one may come with you..."). Instruct your children to cherish time alone with God. Make sure there are no distractions—no competing activities that would draw their attention from God. Turn off the television, radio, computer, and even the telephone. Encourage adult family members to exercise some quiet time in support of the children.

★ **Call out to Him in prayer** ("Call out his name . . ."). If your children learn to begin their quiet time with prayer, they will establish a lifelong habit of surrendering to the will of God. Prayer puts one's heart in a disposition of submission and obedience. Children need a great deal of encouragement in obedience on a daily basis.

★ **Listen to His voice** ("Then he passed in front of Moses, calling out . . ."). Teach your children that reading the Bible is the same as listening to the voice of God. The Scriptures are God's words to mankind. Explain to your little ones that the Word of God is to be taken very personally and very seriously. Emphasize that it is not merely a history book or a book of facts. The Bible is a love letter written from God to man. And most important—it calls for a response.

> How, then, do you begin? You need only one thing. You need only to know how to seek Him. When you have found the way to seek Him, you will discover that this way to God is more natural and easier than taking a breath.
>
> -Jeanne Guyon

75

★ **Worship** ("Immediately, Moses knelt, bowing his face touching the ground . . ."). Finally, teach your children to worship God in their daily quiet time. There are so many ways to worship. One child may elect to write her sentiments in a journal. Another may prefer to end in a prayer. One child might decide on a course of action that should be taken in worshipful response. Another might simply say, "Thank you, Jesus," as he finishes his devotions. You can assist your children in worship by providing a tape or CD player. Allow them to choose songs that correspond to their readings or those that they simply enjoy.

Your children can reflect the glory of God and radiate the love of Christ by developing the habit of "stealing away" with God.

Moses had an amazing, life-altering experience on the mountain that day. He descended from the meeting place with radiance so bright that the children of Israel were frightened to look at him. Likewise, your children can reflect the glory of God and radiate the love of Christ by developing the habit of "stealing away" with God.

You Can Do It!
Enhancing Healthy Independence and Self-Discipline

Most parents start out with grand aspirations concerning what they want their children to do when they grow up: be a doctor, lawyer, or astronaut; but not a mechanic, tree-trimmer, or bank teller. About how they should live: in an upscale suburb, with a three-car garage; not a grass hut on the mission field. Who they should marry: the valedictorian of the graduating class, the son or daughter of a dignitary; not the offspring of a blue-collar worker. And what kind of person they will turn out to be: magnanimous, heroic, CEO material; not quiet, reserved, and meek.

Most parents discover sometime during the teen years that those aspirations might have been a little off the mark. Their children have their own ideas, their own preferences, their own interests, and their own aspirations about how to spend the lives laid out before them.

Often, there is tension between parent and child as the years pass and reality begins to set in.

A fascinating example in the Scriptures was Samson, one of

the judges of Israel. Born to a man named Manoah, Samson just didn't turn out the way his parents had envisioned him. In fact, Manoah's wife was barren. An angel appeared to announce that a child was coming—it was to be an act of God. He said, "You will become pregnant and give birth to a son, and his hair must never be cut. For he will be dedicated to God . . . from birth. He will rescue Israel from the Philistines" (Judges 13:5 NLT).

If they were typical as parents, Mr. and Mrs. Manoah probably had a grandiose expectation about Samson growing up to be an outstanding Israelite—a man who would stand head and shoulders above all others in character; a man who would lead the nation in righteousness and peace. But Samson turned out to be a real surprise. He broke every vow related to his dedication, was prone to hang out with prostitutes, was a trickster and an agitator, had a reputation for brutality, and couldn't keep his eyes off the women he wasn't supposed to marry—the enemy's female constituency. Wherever Samson went, trouble was sure to follow. Neither was he known as a team player. Manoah would surely have been proud of him had he lead a great army. Samson preferred to single-handedly take down the masses with the skulls of asses.

Yet in all that Samson was—and wasn't—he managed to fulfill the mission that the Almighty had put upon his heart.

Perhaps the best thing you can do is to equip your children with a responsible and healthy independence, follow up with the development of self-discipline, which will ensure that they fulfill their own aspirations, and then stay out of the way. In so doing, you'll signal to your children that you have confidence in their ability to discern the path they need to take. They, in turn, will feel cherished and respected, probably remaining more open to your opinions and counsel since you have given them the latitude to exercise their own options.

Perhaps the best thing you can do is to equip your children with a responsible and healthy independence.

How can you help your children develop independence and self-discipline? Volumes have been written on this subject by experts with many degrees of education and experience. Many tried-and-true strategies for success are available for your perusal. However, your common sense will take you a long way down this path. Try the following suggestions as a springboard. Teach your children to:

★ Start with a vision.

★ Take responsibility.

★ Set a goal.

★ Make a plan.

★ Learn to say "yes" to opportunity and interruptions.

★ Learn to say "no" to distractions and unnecessary diversions.

★ Make room for the vision beyond self.

The process of developing these life skills can be invigorating and provide many opportunities for your relationship to flourish.

Start with a vision. Children come into the age of responsibility and accountability at various ages, depending on their understanding and maturity level. When you perceive that your child has "come of age," you might want to set aside an evening wherein you can discuss the vision that is formulating within the child's mind about who he is to be. Scheduling a private dinner out, for instance, would leave the appropriate impression that her future is of great importance to you.

One good way to approach the discussion is simply to ask: "Who do you want to be?" That is not the same as asking, "What do you want to do?" That distinction needs to be clarified. In our culture, we tend to define people first by their occupation. It is an unfortunate perversion of values. Stress the importance of defining oneself by character rather than by occupation.

> A person's character and their garden both
> reflect the amount of weeding that
> was done in the growing season.
> **-Author Unknown**

Take responsibility. The question relevant to this discussion is: "What will I need to do to get there?" This is the preparatory work for setting goals. The important principle involved in this discussion has to do with taking responsibility for results.

> The first requisite of a good citizen
> in this Republic of ours
> is that he shall be able and
> willing to pull his weight.
> **-Theodore Roosevelt**

Set a goal. Your children must learn that the only progress that will be made is the progress that is planned for. Goals need to be reasonable, reachable, and respectable.

> First build a proper goal.
> That proper goal will make it easy,
> almost automatic, to build a proper you.
> **-Goethe**

Make a plan. For each goal set, there must be a strategy laid out in order to accomplish it.

Perhaps the most valuable result of all education is the ability to make yourself do the thing you have to do when it ought to be done whether you like it or not. It is the first lesson that ought to be learned . . . It is probably the last lesson a person learns thoroughly.
-Thomas Huxley

—•—

Learn to say "yes" to opportunity and interruptions. Opportunities are rarely of the "silver spoon" variety. It isn't often that the opportunity matches up specifically with the goal. There is great value in learning to look for the indirect benefits of each opportunity. And it is important to note that opportunity often comes packaged as problems and challenges, rather than as "offers" and "invitations." Meanwhile, learning to accept interruptions teaches your children to value people over tasks. They need to learn to prioritize the needs of others over the accomplishment of any ideal.

No one of us is more important than the rest of us.
-Ray Kroc

—•—

Learn to say "no" to distractions and unnecessary diversions. Children fall prey to all sorts of diversions—video games, friends who have no goals, bad habits. To teach this skill is to teach discernment and discretion. The old saying is, "Opportunity costs," and your sons or daughters will need to learn to make wise choices. Applaud them for the good ones!

Destiny is not a matter of chance,
it is a matter of choice;
it is not a thing to be waited for,
it is a thing to be achieved.

-William J. Bryan

—•—

Make room for the vision beyond self. The most neglected principle in learning independence and self-discipline is the lesson of humility. Unless your children learn that the world does not revolve around them, that they must treat others with the respect and value that they hope to receive, and that their aspirations fit circumspectly into a larger picture—God's picture—they will not achieve a healthy independence nor personal discipline.

When we learn to place proper value
on other people, we can be sure our values
have been properly placed.

-Author Unknown

Gifts and Callings
Helping Your Kids Discover Their God-Given Gifts and Callings

You know them—those people who hate customer service, yet work in a customer-service industry; those teachers who don't have much tolerance for children, but have been teaching for thirty years; those salesmen who are too introverted to pitch their product, but too shy to interview for another job; those publishers who never read, but try to stay ahead of the market; those brokers who can't manage their own investments, but make bold promises concerning other people's money; and those public speakers with monotone voices and minimal gestures, who persist in the public arena.

Every occupation suffers the mistaken employ of men and women who are not suited to execute its function. It bears the same sore effect as would walking in a shoe that doesn't fit. You expend a lot of time, become frustrated over the wear and tear, and suffer through a great deal of pain—yet you don't get very far.

One young woman wanted desperately to become a marine biologist, but she suffered from an inordinate fear of sharks and alligators. Another young man wanted a musical career in the entertainment industry, but his voice was so bad, his dog ran and hid under the bed whenever he started to sing.

The same principle holds true concerning one's role in the kingdom of God. Unrelated to occupation—though not mutually exclusive—every believer has a purpose assigned to them by the Almighty, a purpose only they can fulfill in this life. In determining that purpose, or calling, one must first determine with which gifts he has been equipped. Where there are no gifts, there is no calling. In whatever dimension the gifts are manifest, therein will be the calling. You will bless your children immensely if you can help them to understand this profound spiritual principle.

> **God's gifts and God's call are under full warranty**
> **—never canceled, never rescinded.**
>
> **ROMANS 11:29** MSG

Take time to teach your children about their "gifts and callings."

The first step in determining your child's gifts involves observation. What are his natural strengths in dealing with people?

Does she have an unusually compassionate heart? Is he a friend to the downtrodden? How about organizational skills? Does she prefer to supervise everyone else? Does he always see the potential in situations and people, utilizing his imagination to launch grandiose adventures and schemes? Or does your child see the problems with every endeavor—scrutinizing with natural analytical skills; given to detail?

The first step in determining your child's gifts involves observation.

Your children should be helpful in determining their strengths. They know what holds their interest and what doesn't. People are usually gifted in areas of greatest interest. They know in what situations they feel confident and when they don't.

Sometimes confidence can help in discerning gifts. Once you've determined that you have discovered some areas wherein your children have exceptional abilities, encourage them in those things. However, it is advisable to keep the door open to the possibility that things might evolve differently than you expect. Once fully mature, a child may experience the spontaneous development of another type of gift—one that wasn't discernable initially.

Second, it is prudent to help your children determine their weaknesses as well. Every strength has a corresponding and proportionate weakness. If, for instance, your daughter is extremely merciful, she may also be extremely gullible—easily taken advantage of. If your son is analytical and scrutinizing, he may struggle with the tendency to become critical and negative. Whatever the weakness, it will mirror the child's strength in intensity and ineffectiveness. Whatever glory might have gone to God will be tarnished before delivery if the child's weaknesses are not dealt with.

Weaknesses should not become a focal point, but rather a

point of honest self-evaluation from time to time. Then, if any red flag is raised, your child's first recourse will be to step back and evaluate the problem, considering his own propensities and weaknesses at the front end. She will learn to be more objective and more effective if she keeps her own weaknesses in perspective.

> **Face the facts, but don't dwell on the facts; dwell on what you want them to become.**
>
> -William Lantz

After discovering their gifts, your children need to understand that they must be developed and practiced. Encourage your youngsters to be creative in expressing their talents and abilities. Applaud them in their successes and console them when they experience failure and discouragement.

Once the gifts have been determined, you can help open doors to their minds concerning what possibilities might be considered in answering their callings from God. Take note of your child's interest in different areas of Christian service. The gifts naturally fall into one of two categories: speaking or serving gifts.

God has given gifts to each of you from his great variety of spiritual gifts. Manage them well so that God's generosity can flow through you. Are you called to be a speaker? Then speak as though God himself were speaking through you. Are you called to help others? Do it with all the strength and energy that God supplies. Then God will be given glory in everything through Jesus Christ.

1 PETER 4:10-11 NLT

One child may show more interest in service projects than in learning to teach cradle roll. Perhaps he aspires to a missionary campaign in middle school or prefers to help rake leaves for a widow or elderly neighbor.

As your children grow, pray with them about their callings and the purpose that God has determined for their gifts and abilities. Let those prayers become a springboard for further discussion and discovery.

> *As your children grow,*
> *pray with them about their callings.*

Finally, teach your children by example that their gifts are from God and are intended to be shared with other people. Giftedness is a delight to the soul of him upon whom the gift falls, but it is intended for the benefit of others. Model the generosity that is fitting for the people of God, who is himself lavish with His blessings. Teach your children to be lavish with God's blessings through them. Instruct them to develop the habit of saying "yes" to service opportunities as often as they can. Then you will know that you have built into the fiber of each child's existence a disposition toward helping other people and a sensitivity to God's calling.

> There is something that is much more scarce, something far finer, something rarer than ability. It is the ability to recognize ability.
> **-Elbert Hubbard**

85

In summary, when addressing the biblical concept of spiritual gifts:

- ★ Teach them to know their strengths—and develop them.

- ★ Teach them to know their weaknesses—and watch for them.

- ★ Teach them to seek God's will—and put their gifts to use.

- ★ Teach them to give their gifts lavishly and as often as called upon.

Lifting Holy Hands to God
Helping Your Kids Appreciate and Participate in Corporate Worship

One little girl sat in the church service, singing the old hymn "Low in the Grave He Lay." The chorus as penned says:

Up from the grave, He arose!
With a mighty triumph oe'r His foes.

At the top of her lungs, her version went as follows:
Up from the gravy ... a rose!
With a mighty trumpet on its toes!

Humorous, yes! Uncommon, no! This innocent misappropriation of worship illustrates a common problem; or perhaps it would be more correct to say: a common misunderstanding. The little girl was actually imaging her mother's gravy boat chock-full of dark beef gravy, when suddenly a beautiful rose emerges from the abyss of the bowl and ascends above the table in radiance and splendor. And alas! Fastened to its root structure, an impressive brass instrument heralds its appearance and glorification—a mighty trumpet playing some majestic rendition of "The Yellow Rose of Texas."

The experience of worship for a child can be just that ignorant and confused. So how can you help your children learn the truth about worship? Begin by listening to the words of Jesus as He spoke them to an "ignorant" individual of his day:

The time is coming when the true worshipers will worship the Father in spirit and truth, and that time is here already. You see, the Father too is actively seeking such people to worship him.

JOHN 4:23 NCV

Try teaching these simple, yet profound, principles that Jesus taught.

★ Worship of the Father

★ Worship in Spirit

★ True Worship

★ The Father Is Seeking

Worship of the Father. The most critical lesson with which to impress the heart and mind of your children is that God is not just God—Creator, Omnipotent, Omniscient, Omnipresent—but that God is their Father. This was the most striking claim Jesus ever made—calling the Almighty His "Father." The religious experts of the day were up in arms over the implications of that statement. Yet to Jesus, His Sonship was neither a statement of arrogance nor a claim to position. It was an honest statement about submission and trust. Jesus came to reveal God as a loving Father. He came to reorient the people's perception of their God—to make their faith relational instead of institutional.

> *The most critical lesson with which to impress the heart and mind of your children is that God is their Father.*

In other words, He came to show mankind how to crawl up into the lap of the Almighty and speak to Him as a child would to a father. The title with which Jesus addressed God—Abba—is the word Hebrew children used to address their own fathers. It meant "Daddy," and it references His intimacy, dependency, and the complete surrender to God, His Father.

Teach your children, by your example, that God is Father, and worship is not the "act" or "form" by which one engages God. Worship is to enter into the actual presence of the Father God and incline one's heart to His face. The "acts" or "forms" are important only because they are vehicles that can carry us into God's presence. But the "forms" themselves are of no value if the heart is never really lifted into an expression of praise and petition to the Almighty.

God has two thrones:
one in the highest heaven;
the other is in the lowliest heart.
-Author Unknown

Worship in Spirit. The spirit of the worshiper is critical to true worship. Help your children cultivate an expectancy—an anticipation—of the Father's presence. This is the disposition of spirit that Jesus modeled: "I always do what is pleasing to him, so he has not left me alone" (John 8:29 NCV). The spirit of a true worshiper is the spirit of sonship or the spirit of submission. The heart rendered to God as Father—trusting Him, obeying Him, relying upon Him, following Him, living for Him, working in His kingdom—is the heart that the Father recognizes as His own.

A common mistake among believing people is the practice of showing up for church services, participating in the "acts of worship," and then leaving to resume one's self-centered pursuits. It is like punching a time clock: "I've validated my parking place in heaven, so back to living for myself." Attending church services and going through the motions of worship does not ensure that worship occurs. Another common misunderstanding is the thought that an emotional response to spiritual entertainment is the same as true worship. The spirit of worship isn't the extreme to which your emotions can carry you on the wings of an upbeat "praise and worship" song. The spirit of worship is the extent to which your heart is impressed with the need to submit your whole existence to the Father who loves you.

> God is not moved or impressed
> with our worship until our hearts are
> moved and impressed by Him.
> **-Kelly Sparks**

True Worship. True worship is real worship. The truth about worship is the grace that brought mankind into a relationship with God to begin with. The true worshiper has a very real awareness of his need for redemptive grace—the forgiveness of God, the power of God, the provision of God, and hope in God. Teaching your children about true worship means teaching him to keep his true identity in proper perspective as he considers the true identity of the Father he is worshiping. It is humble, grateful, expressive, life-changing, inspiring, and honest.

Worship requires only a man and God.

True worship takes into account not only that the child has been saved by the grace of God, but that he is sustained and delivered daily by the grace of God. It isn't just worship for past redemption; it is adoration for today's rescue. It isn't just praise for deeds done; it is gratitude for what is yet to come. True worship anticipates the blessing of the Father, takes into consideration the mission of the Father, and expresses heartfelt intentions about relationship with the Father.

> To believe God is to worship God.
> **-Martin Luther**

The Father Is Seeking. One more consideration suggested by Jesus in this text is that the Father is actively seeking these true spiritual worshipers. How inspiring and encouraging for your children to realize that their efforts are not a feeble attempt to reach up to a faraway God. They are looking to a Father who already has them in His sights. Even their attempts are His idea.

What does that mean? It means He is seeking all who worship

Him in this way. He is seeking a family of worshipers, and your children learn a healthy respect and appreciation for all whom the Lord is seeking. He meets His worshipers more than halfway. The Father is truly a father—assisting your children in every way that a father would—making himself accessible, approachable, available, and responsive. Your children need to have an image of the Almighty Abba searching the room for their faces and lighting up once their eyes have connected; kneeling down to take them into His gracious arms, and holding them close as they worship.

> Salvation is wholly of grace, not only undeserved but undesired by us until God is pleased to awaken us to a sense of our need of it. And then we find everything prepared that our wants require or our wishes conceive; yea, that He has done exceedingly beyond that we could either ask or think. Salvation is wholly of the Lord and bears those signatures of infinite wisdom, power, and goodness which distinguish all His works from the puny imitations of men. It is every way worthy of Himself, a great, a free, a full, a sure salvation.
>
> -John Newton

This is the context in which the heart finds expression through the body. Your children's expression of worship should be as free as it is in their love for their earthly father. They should feel free to experience celebration, awe, sorrow, and joy. They should be encouraged to be themselves before the Lord, not crammed into a worship mold that doesn't fit them at all. They should find themselves smiling, shouting, kneeling, dancing, clapping, crying, and laughing—all in honest response to a loving Father.

Admittedly, it would be quite an experience to see a rose ascend from the depths of a gravy boat with a trumpet blasting in announcement; but one would have to question just how beneficial it would be to one's spirit.

90

But the fact that Jesus arose from a grave! Now that will cause your spirit to worship—truly!

Unto Others
Teaching Your Kids Creative Ways to Show Love and Respect for Others

Children are highly sensory individuals—refreshingly alive to touch, smell, sight, sound, and taste. Because of that, they find creativity in the context of sensory expressions easy to come by.

"Look, Mom, I drew you a picture!" (sight)

"Do you like the flowers I picked for you?" (smell)

"Daddy, I made some cookies just for you." (taste)

"I'll give you a hug to make you feel better." (touch)

"Would you like me to sing you a song?" (hearing)

You can put their acute sensitivity to their sensory organs to work while learning to express love and respect in creative ways.

Expressions you can see.

A little boy said to his daddy, "I love you with my eyes, Dad."

"What do you mean?" his father asked.

"I mean, every time my eyes see you, my heart loves you," he responded profoundly.

A great deal of love and respect is communicated through sight. One very effective way that children can learn to express respect is to be attentive with their eyes when someone is speaking to them.

A great deal of love and respect is communicated through sight.

Children find it challenging to be still enough, long enough. Everything within them cries "Action!" If you teach your children to pay respect to others by being fully engaged when in conversation, people—particularly adults—will love to be in their company.

Teach your children to master their bodies, learning to sit or stand quietly, while letting their eyes do the action. It is important, however, that children learn the difference between genuine attentiveness and a rude stare. One is endearing; the other is unnerving.

Expressions you can hear.

A teacher was having difficulty with one little girl who refused to accept her authority in the classroom. She instructed the seven-year-old to refer to her as "Ma'am," saying, "That just sounds more respectful."

"That's not what respect sounds like," the little girl replied, refusing to do as requested.

The teacher then asked the girl: "Well, Regina, what does respect sound like?"

"I don't know," Regina shot back. "I ain't never heard it."

Another genuine expression of love and respect comes from the tone of your voice. The human voice is much like a fine instrument. If played recklessly and without concern for pitch or practice, it may be unpleasant and discordant. But if you teach your children to inflect their voices intentionally—considerate of the situation they are in—people will feel respected, as well as be drawn to them in conversation.

Another genuine expression of love and respect comes from the tone of your voice.

Expressions you can taste.

"Mom, I wish you loved me as much as Tommy's mom loves him," six-year-old Michael said.

"What do you mean?" Michael's mom was shocked and concerned.

"When I was eating supper over there the other night, Tommy said to his mom, 'Mom, why do you cook so good?' Then Tommy's mom said back: "Cause I love you so much.'"

"So what is your point, Michael?" his mother pressed.

"You hardly cook at all, and when you do, it isn't anything like Tommy's mom!"

The old saying goes, "The way to a man's heart is through his stomach." There is some truth to that—however, not just applicable to men. Jesus often fed people and dined with them. There is something about good food and good drink that sweetens relationships.

A creative way to express love and respect is to prepare tasty delights. But teach your children some new and unconventional ideas for a fresh wave of communication:

★ Stack some marshmallows at each person's place when having a family meeting or when it's time for homework. Marshmallows can serve to sweeten any discussion or may be used as an armory if someone feels the need to "drop a bomb" on somebody else.

★ Serve a cup of crushed ice with some really strong lemonade for an afternoon treat while Dad is mowing the lawn. The lemonade will dilute as the ice melts, making a delicious and refreshing treat while cleansing the palate of dust.

★ Put a dollop of vanilla ice cream in a cup of hot chocolate for a cozy autumn evening around the fireplace.

★ Encourage your children to be creative and think up new ways of doing "old favorites" in order to communicate love and appreciation for family members and friends.

Thoughtful gifts from the heart make love tangible.

94

Expressions you can smell.

Taylor asked her mom, "How come you only love Daddy when he smells good?"

"I don't!" her mom answered defensively. "Why would you think that?"

"Last night, after Daddy's softball game, he tried to hug you and you pushed him away. You said, 'Huh-uh! You stink!'"

Love is easy through the olfactory senses! In fact, experts say that your sense of smell stimulates memories more profoundly than any other sense. It can be so much fun to surprise people with fragrance. Teach your children these fragrant offerings of love and respect:

★ Give Mom a small pot of rosemary to grow in the kitchen.

★ Buy Sister some natural soaps and oils for bathing.

★ Hang dried lavender flowers in a cotton sock in Grandma's closet.

★ Hang sheets on a clothesline outside to dry.

★ Help Mom light scented candles after dinner.

★ Have a freshly brewed pot of coffee prepared when Dad wakes up.

Expressions you can feel.

"I don't like to hug Uncle Norm," Sam said to his sister.

"Why? He's a good uncle."

"Because his neck won't bend and my head doesn't have anybody to touch."

Jesus believed in touch because people need touching. Perhaps nothing communicates love as much as an authentic hug; and surely nothing is more respectful than a hearty handshake. Children need to learn loving and respectful ways to stay "in touch" with their human fellows.

The most important lesson you can teach your children about love and respect is that it is returned in proportion to how it is given. The more loving a person is toward others—regardless of how lovable people are—the more loved that person will be. The more respect a person pays to others—no matter whether they are worthy of respect—the more respected that person will be. In fact, love and respect come back to you heaped up, piled on, shaken down, and running over!

An Attitude of Gratitude
Helping Your Kids Develop Grateful Hearts

**Be cheerful no matter what; pray all the time;
thank God no matter what happens.**

1 THESSALONIANS 5:16-18 MSG

These words of the apostle Paul promote a wonderful philosophy for living. However wonderful, they are very difficult to put into practice.

Take for instance:

★ The day you left for work a little late and traffic was backed up for a mile on the main thoroughfare due to an accident. Be cheerful, you say?

★ The day you answered the front door to discover a policeman holding your son's elbow in one hand, your son's BB gun in the other. You suggest prayer? Pray what? That the windshield through which he just shot a hole will somehow miraculously mend?

★ The time your neighbor asked you to baby-sit her cocker spaniel, forgetting to mention that the dog chews leather shoes and purses—only the finest of leather—not to mention alligator and ostrich, too. (Pretty much everything in your closet except your canvas sneakers that you bought at a sidewalk sale for $9.98.) Give thanks? You mean, for the cocker spaniel, or for the friend who forgot to warn you?

★ Or maybe it was the night you had the boss and his wife over for dessert and coffee. You know, the night you burned the crepes and remembered—after they had consumed the coffee—that they can't have caffeine.

★ Or finally, the time you waited four weeks for that really cute coat to go on sale—the belted one with the pleats in the back bodice—and you stood for fifteen minutes, waiting for the doors to unlock at the "early bird" opening, yet as you were running for it, you witnessed the last one fly off the rack into someone's possession and out the door.

Being able to maintain a gratitude attitude in difficult circumstances is a sign of spiritual maturity.

Be cheerful? Pray? Be thankful?

The fact is, being thankful is just easier said than done. And you already know, the same will hold true for your children.

If you are like most people, you won't have difficulty teaching your children to be thankful when everything is going their way; they'll pick up on it pretty quickly. It's the issue of not having their way that will present a challenge. So what is the answer? What should you teach your children about thankfulness?

The apostle Paul gave a formula for the cheerful, prayerful attitude of gratitude that he described earlier. To make the point more vivid, he penned the following words from a prison cell:

> **I don't have a sense of needing anything personally. I've learned by now to be quite content whatever my circumstances. I'm just as happy with little as with much, with much as with little. I've found the recipe for being happy whether full or hungry, hands full or hands empty. Whatever I have, wherever I am, I can make it through anything in the One who makes me who I am.**
>
> PHILIPPIANS 4:11-13 MSG

Slow down and really digest what he means by all of that.

Whatever the circumstances—little or much—acknowledge God's provision.

For most people, circumstances dictate mood. If the weather is gloomy, so are they. If finances are strained, so are they. If their spouse is mad, so are they. Children are less reactive to circumstances in their moods, probably because they don't understand the implications of the situations they find themselves in. However, your children will likely grow into the tendency to be managed by what is going on around them, unless you help them learn that their resources are not from without—they are from within.

Gratitude doesn't come from outside gratification; it comes

from within. It doesn't come from getting what you hope for, but from being complete no matter what happens. By example, you can teach your children how to appreciate the provisions that God has made and how to rely upon the providence of God for the future. It all depends upon your outlook. Your children will learn from you, as eyewitnesses, whether God is truly adequate when everything doesn't work out the way you had hoped. In those times you have the opportunity to teach them that going without some things may even be the provision of God.

Gratitude doesn't come from outside gratification, it comes from within.

That's why we can be so sure that every detail in our lives of love for God is worked into something good.

ROMANS 8:28 MSG

Discover the recipe for being happy; accept the peace of God.

The key ingredient to gratitude is contentment. Contentment comes from finding peace with God, peace in God, and as a result, peace with yourself and your circumstances. You can teach your children this kind of peace by looking for the greater purpose in both abundance and adversity.

Strange as it may seem, children have just as much difficulty with contentment in the midst of great prosperity as they do in times of want—sometimes more. The constant craving for more—more things, more entertainment, more recreation—can become almost addictive. The more a child gets, the more the child wants. There is so much to be gained in learning the peace that comes from denying oneself instant gratification in every situation. Your children will learn to be content with life at a deeper level than mere desire can afford. Contentment is a powerful state of mind that produces genuine gratitude.

Contentment is a powerful state of mind that produces genuine gratitude.

You can make it through anything; tap into the power of God.

You can teach your children to be thankful in any situation by discovering the power that is within them if they will turn to Jesus. Teach your children by your example that gratitude begins with a prayerful disposition. Show your children how to thank God personally for all that He has already provided; your youngsters will discover great strength in rehearsing the many blessings that God has given them up to now. Faith springs to life within the hearts of those who confess God's power and goodness in prayer. Before the praying is ended, your children's hearts will be shorn up with the confidence that God always has and always will provide.

I am ready for anything through the strength of the one who lives within me.

PHILIPPIANS 4:13 PHILLIPS

Believe in the One who makes you what you are; be aware that you are in the presence of God.

The One who is able to sustain your children through any circumstance, any hardship, any trial, and any joy is Jesus. And one of the greatest gifts of all is the individual whom God made when He made each of your children. It is critical to the process of maturing that your children learn to be grateful for who they are in the eyes of God. Learning to be grateful for their own existence in the presence of the Almighty is rudimentary to all other aspects of contentment and ultimately gratitude.

Instruct your children in giving thanks not only for what they consider their assets, but for those things they consider their liabilities, as well. The grace of God is manifested in His people through their weakness, not just through their strengths. He makes himself evident in the lives of each of your children in ways they would never suspect. Help your children learn to verbalize those things.

And most importantly, teach your children that in the presence of God, they are as precious children—valued by God Almighty as His most cherished possessions—and for that, they should be grateful.

> **God loved the world so much that he gave his one and only Son so that whoever believes in him may not be lost, but have eternal life.**
>
> **JOHN 3:16 NCV**

The world should thank Him for that!

A Friend Indeed!
Teaching Your Kids the Art of Developing Godly Friendships

If you haven't already, you will eventually discover that one of the toughest and touchiest aspects of parenting concerns the friendships of your children. Every parent knows what it is to experience the dismay, fear, and heartache associated with difficult friendships.

A faithful friend is an image of God.

How can you encourage your children to be drawn to good people? The answer to that question could make a person rich and famous, for it has eluded parents from the beginning of time. Here are some things to consider:

Spend time in intentional, instructional, and inspiring discussions about friendships before your children start school.

Six months before each of your children begins school—as his or her anticipation is building toward the big event—teach your child the basics about friendship. Repetition is key to learning; however, this is one lesson you don't want to harp about. Some good stories from your own experiences as a child—both happy and not-so-happy—will provide the perfect springboard for these spontaneous opportunities.

Be certain that your teaching focuses on the issues of character, values, and common sense. Discuss the common ground that one finds in a person with common values. Pray with your children about their discernment, about self-respect and respect for others, and finally, about God's will in their lives concerning friendship.

Keep an open mind and heart.

When your children actually do make friends, have an open mind about who they are. Express a genuine interest in their friends and their friends' families—what they like to do, how they treat other people, and what the friendship has to offer each party.

As soon as possible, have your children's friends into your home so that you can establish a relationship with them yourself. The more interest you demonstrate toward their friends, the more interested your children will be in your opinion. Not to mention that you'll be able to make a much better judgment at close range.

Children get defensive when their parents make snap judgments about someone that they are attracted to and vice versa. In fact, the more adamant the parent is in expressing opposition to the friendship, the more determined your children may become.

> Every child that is born comes with a message that God is not yet discouraged with mankind.
> —**Rabindranath Tagore**

They may feel the need to protect their newfound comrades from the daggers of their critical family members. They could end up seeking and finding safer refuge with the very people you are trying to protect them from.

Trust your children to exercise good judgment and make a genuine attempt to understand what they see in any person they have befriended.

102

Keep in mind that you are helping your children construct a worldview about people in general.

What you communicate to your children concerning friendships will make a lasting impression upon their hearts and actions throughout their lives. You should be very careful to avoid any instruction that could communicate prejudice or bias toward or against any particular type of people or segment of society. Teaching your children the principles of humility and integrity will fortify them with better judgment and skill than all that pride and prejudice has to offer.

> When a man begins to realize the truth about himself, it often retards his plan for reforming his neighbors.
> —**Author Unknown**

As you instruct your children about making friends, you are also constructing their worldview. Their perceptions concerning their role among people will be formulated from this early beginning. That awareness will sober you to pray about what God's will is in the matter. Maybe the Lord prefers that a certain child is associated with your youngster, spending time in your home, and under your influence. Consider it a blessing when your child brings home someone whom you feel compelled to pray for. That could be intentional, for in some cases, unless you pray, no one will.

Be aware that the will of God may not back up your opinion concerning the friendship.

Long ago, in ancient Israel, there was a king who had strong opinions about his son's choice of friends. The king was Saul, his son was Jonathan, and the friend was David the shepherd boy. King Saul held David in contempt because he was a threat to Jonathan's throne. He tried repeatedly to warn Jonathan that he was putting his own future at risk, even going to the extreme of trying to murder David himself, but Jonathan loved David and was fulfilling a calling much higher, much nobler, than merely his status.

As difficult as it is to accept, one or all of your children might be singled out by the Almighty as an ambassador to someone. It is sheer arrogance that assumes the Lord always agrees with you about the people you don't like. And has it ever crossed your mind that He cares about what happens to the children you don't want your children associating with?

If you lose sight of the mission, your children will have a very difficult time keeping it in sight. Teach them to love all others, to be kind and compassionate to all.

*Teach your children to love all others,
to be kind and compassionate to all.*

God has chosen you and made you his holy people. He loves you. So always do these things: Show mercy to others, be kind, humble, gentle, and patient.

COLOSSIANS 3:12 NCV

Teach your children to be faithful witnesses.

The most critical lesson you can teach your children, once their selection of friends has been made, is to keep Jesus in the

No one is more confusing than the fellow who gives good advice while setting a bad example.

—Author Unknown

center of the friendship. The youngsters should be encouraged to open their hearts to all, while remaining uncompromising in their loyalty to God.

Your examples in friendship will be the most profound lessons your children will learn.

104

Choosing the Good
Helping Your Kids Make Godly Decisions

**Hold on to wisdom, and it will take care of you.
Love it, and it will keep you safe.**

PROVERBS 4:6 NCV

Everyone faces the difficulty involved with making decisions. Good decisions can put your feet on a path of success and fulfillment in relationships, occupation, spiritual well-being, and in eternity. Bad ones may send you reeling into despair, struggling to keep your head above water, and spending the rest of your life trying to repair broken relationships and a shattered reputation.

Decisions can take you out of God's will but never out of His reach.

The good news is that diligence in decision making can ensure good results. The bad news? Diligence isn't as gratifying in the short run as greed, pleasure, and power. Most poor decisions are like that—baited with one or more of those temptations.

Children can be taught while very young how to develop the skills for making godly decisions. It is of the utmost importance that those doing the teaching have learned and implemented these skills in their own lives. Otherwise, because your actions speak louder than your words, the lesson will be lost on the hearer.

One of the writers of the New Testament penned some words about using wisdom in making life's most pressing decisions. He said:

The wisdom that comes from heaven is first of all pure. It is also peace loving, gentle at all times, and willing to yield to others. It is full of mercy and good deeds. It shows no partiality and is always sincere.

JAMES 3:17 NLT

The following principles will prove most helpful in instructing your children in making decisions that will honor the Lord and lead to joyful and fulfilling lives. Teach them to:

★ Consider the motive

★ Consider the counsel of others

★ Consider those who will be directly affected

★ Do what is right, regardless

★ Be merciful

★ Be real

★ Have integrity

No matter what the decision, these principles (where applicable) will keep your children's hearts and minds on the right path—the path of wisdom.

Consider the motive. Your children will be at an advantage if they learn to stop to make honest evaluation of their own motives. This simple step can fend off devastating decisions. Any motive that is purely selfish should be held suspect—there simply must be more to justify any action than mere selfishness. The key is to teach your children to examine their motives thoroughly in prayer. Once motive is established, clarity comes to the rest of the process. Make them first of all self-aware.

> Learn the art of being aware; our success depends upon our power to perceive, to observe, and know. Keen observation is a chief factor in the success of all great businessmen, executives, artists and military leaders.
> **Henry Miller**

106

Consider the counsel of others. The most important counsel your children can seek is the counsel of the Almighty. Spending some time in the Word of God can help to bend one's heart to the will of the Lord. He should have the first word on every matter. The Proverbs and the New Testament are chock-full of insights and wisdom. A good concordance or study Bible can aid you and your children in finding scriptures relevant to the decision they are making.

The most important counsel your children can seek is the counsel of the Almighty.

Depending upon how critical the decision is, how many people it affects, and how far-reaching its implications will be—particularly spiritual implications—the feedback and advice of some trusted friend or family member may also prove invaluable. Asking for the feedback or advice of a trusted individual has a double-edged benefit. First, the exercise of having to verbalize it in an orderly sequence of thought can help a child evaluate whether he or she is being reasonable. Sometimes merely hearing himself talk can help your child see where his reasoning falls short. Second, having been an interested and objective sounding board, the friend or family member has the leverage to help direct your child toward a better resolution.

Consider those who will be directly affected. If the decision will have a direct impact on anyone else's life, it should be taken into serious consideration. Teach your children that it isn't acceptable to rationalize away their responsibility concerning the well-being of other people. It may be advisable to discuss with those potentially affected, asking their input and winning their trust. When your children grow into adults, they will stand out as unselfish individuals who genuinely look after the best interests of others before themselves.

Do what is right, regardless. Instruct your children that no matter what, they must never violate the commands of God, their own consciences, or the rights of others. No temptation for greatness, prosperity, or power is worth compromising your conscience. Teach your children that unless they can look God in the eye with a pure heart, they are headed down the wrong path.

Many think that just a little wrongdoing won't matter in the long run. Instruct your youngsters to resist this rationale and realize that compromising little things now leads to bigger compromises later. The end result will be misery and heartache.

Be merciful. If your children's decisions fall into the category of what to do in relationships, teach them to take the high road and always choose mercy. Many unjust situations will assault them. They will find it tempting to retaliate, to seek revenge. In fact, today's society will encourage them to vindicate themselves and ruin their opponents in the process.

Stress the love and mercy of God—the fact that He gave freely what no man deserves. Instruct your children to imitate God's example and experience the peace of mind that comes with doing so. Teach them to trust the Lord to champion them.

Don't insist on getting even; that's not for you to do. "I'll do the judging," says God. "I'll take care of it."

ROMANS 12:19 MSG

Be real. Teach your youngsters that if the decision requires that they become someone or something other than who they are in the eyes of the Almighty, they should choose the real thing over the "unreal" opportunity. Many people have fallen into the trap of acting out a part they cannot maintain. Sooner or later, the truth will come home to roost. If they have been playing the hypocrite, the mask will get yanked away and humiliation will follow.

Being someone other than who God made you robs the world of one of His gifts.

Have integrity. The issue of integrity lies at the root of all godly decisions. If you teach your children to have integrity before God, with themselves, and with others, their decisions will work out to be the best for their life's journey. Anything that calls them to compromise their convictions, their faith, or their love for their fellowman is less than they were purposed to become. They should be trained to steer clear of those leanings. Jesus made decision making look pretty simple. He said:

I came down from heaven not to follow my own whim but to accomplish the will of the One who sent me.

JOHN 6:38 MSG

If you are successful in transmitting that lesson to your children, you have given them a gift for life!

God's Will—God's Way
Teaching Your Kids Practical Ways to Find God's Will for Their Lives

"Mandy Mae, I told you to be still," her dad scolded. "If you don't obey me, you are going to your room."

"I can't," she shot back.

"What do you mean, you can't?" her dad was growing impatient.

"The Bible says, 'Obey God rather than man,'" she shot back.

"What does that have to do with being still?" he pressed.

"Mama told me that God is inside of me. I tried real hard to be still, but something inside of me is telling me to wiggle. I figure that must be God."

Discerning the will of God is one of the most elusive tasks for anyone—young or old. Unfortunately, children do not come with an instruction manual, complete with specific guidelines for God's will in each child's life. There are, however, specific principles laid out in the Scriptures that will give your children a general idea and put their feet on the right path. Your children can benefit from these reliable biblical principles that will guide them more confidently into seeking the will of God through diligence in prayer.

Discerning the will of God is one of the most elusive tasks for anyone—young or old.

The close friend of Jesus—the apostle Peter—summed these up by saying:

As we know Jesus better, his divine power gives us everything we need for living a godly life. He has called us to receive his

own glory and goodness! And by that same mighty power, he has given us all of his rich and wonderful promises. He has promised that you will . . . share in his divine nature. So make every effort to apply the benefits of these promises to your life. Then your faith will produce a life of moral excellence . . . [which] leads to knowing God better . . . self-control, . . . patient endurance, . . . godliness, . . . love for other Christians, and . . . genuine love for everyone.

2 PETER 1:3-7 NLT

Pursue faith. Help your children develop a vibrant faith by speaking openly and often about Jesus. Children learn best by example and repetition; therefore, making the name of the Lord a common and consistent part of your conversation will teach them to make Him a common consideration and a consistent companion. Faith will give your children the courage to pursue the will of the Lord, regardless of the cost. Pray with your children:

Heavenly Father:
We believe! Please help us when we simply don't believe enough. We want nothing more than to have true faith, living faith, God-honoring faith in you. Lead us to the path where faith will be required of us, so that faith will be secured in us. Amen.

Develop integrity. Teaching by example, discuss your beliefs openly and thoroughly in front of your children, demonstrating how godly people stand firm in their convictions. Point out to them examples where integrity is lacking, being careful not to harm the reputations of others. Learning integrity will help your children sort through lesser options and choose God's will for their lives. Pray with your children:

Father:
In this world of telling lies, cheating, and hurting others, we
want to stand out as people who are different. Instead of
lying, we want to be people of the truth. Instead of cheating,
we want to bless people with our generous ways. Instead of
hurting others, we want to help heal all the broken hearts.
Lead us, Lord, to the liars, the cheaters, and the brokenhearted,
so that we might share Jesus and make a difference in people's
lives.
Amen.

111

Gain spiritual understanding. Knowing God is the most
compelling motive your children will ever experience in pursuing
His will. To know Him is to love Him. Spiritual understanding
comes through time spent in the Word of God—learning not
merely facts, but learning the heart of the Almighty—seeing His
great love through the life and ministry of Jesus. Pray with your
children:

Dear God in Heaven:
Jesus said that we could know you by coming to know Him. It
would be such an awesome thing to know you—really know
you. As we read the Gospels—all that Jesus did, all that He
taught—helps us to see you better. Help us to understand
your nature, your Spirit, and your ways so that we can be your
close friends.
Amen.

Practice self-control. One of the most debilitating things
your children will face as they try to discern the will of God is their
own lack of discipline. Discouragement overtakes the heart when
a child is disappointed in himself. Teach your children to start
with baby steps, and applaud their every effort. Pray with your
children:

Heavenly Father
It is so hard to do the right thing all the time. It is even hard
sometimes to keep from doing wrong. But we know that you
are sad when we are out of control—doing things we
shouldn't, and refusing to do the things we should. We want to
make you proud, Lord. Help us to listen to the inner voice that
tells us the right things to do, and then obey them.
Amen.

Learn patient endurance. In pursuit of God's will, many
obstacles will fly in the face of your children's progress. Prepare
them to expect these setbacks as part of the development of their
faith, teaching them to persist and never give up. Pray with your
children:

Dear Lord:
Living a life of faith can be very difficult. Even when they don't
mean to, people get in the way and trip us up, causing us to
want to quit trying. That is not what we want, Father. Help us
to be stubborn in our love for you and in our determination to
do your will. Help us to know your will without doubting you
in any way. Help us to do your will without fear or embarrass-
ment.
Amen.

Render service to God. In fulfilling the will of God, service
is where the rubber meets the road. Your children need to learn
that faith is only as real as its practice. Faith in action is faith
indeed. Be creative about how to help your children learn the
wonder and fulfillment of service. Volunteer to help in a nursing
home, an orphanage, a children's worship hour. Let your children
be your assistants in service and celebrate together the joy and
peace that comes with doing the will of God. Pray with your children:

Mighty God:
After all the mighty works that you have done for us, we want
to return the favor. Help us, Lord, to search out the ways that
we can serve you that will bring great honor to you and great
joy to others. Help us to do these things with a willing heart
and a cheerful face. We want our greatest deeds to be done in
service to you, not in service to ourselves.
Amen.

113

Show family affection. Loving those who are in the community of faith is the privilege and calling of all believers. Jesus said, "All people will know that you are my followers if you love each other" (John 13:35 NCV). If we do not love our brothers and sisters in faith, we cannot love God, which has obvious and negative implications for accomplishing His will. Pray with your children:

Almighty Abba:
We are aware of your great love—the love of a Father. And we
are aware that your will for us is that we love each other—all
who belong to you—because of your great love. Help us, Lord,
to grow in our love. Help us to love each other as you love us.
Help us, Father, to prove to the world that we believe in you
because of our love for each other.
Amen.

Lavish love on everyone. Finally, in the will of God, the child of God expresses his or her faith by answering His call to love those outside the community of believers. Your children need to know that it is their indiscriminate love for people that will draw them to Jesus. This awareness lends great purpose to every task, every employment, every day of their lives. Pray with your children:

Dear Heavenly Father:
We want to do your will in all things. In particular, we want to

*love the world the way you loved the world when you sent
Jesus to rescue us. He came in love before we were willing to
love Him in return. Help us to love others before they are
willing to love us in return. Help us to love them in such a
powerful way that they come running to you.
Amen.*

The will of God must be sought in prayer—believing prayer,
persistent prayer, heartfelt, passionate prayer.

114

Faithful Stewards
Teaching Your Kids to Be Good Stewards of Their Resources

**Seek first his kingdom and his righteousness, and all these
things will be given to you as well.**

MATTHEW 6:33

Every parent longs to teach his or her children a healthy, balanced perspective concerning money and material possessions. In
addition, every parent hopes that their children will enjoy a comfortable level of success in financial matters. That's why parents
spend so much of their lives preparing their children for their
financial future; while, for most, less emphasis is placed on their
spiritual development.

The problem begins with the fact that an education isn't enough anymore—it has to be the best education money can buy—at a highly accredited school—boasting the highest volume of merit scholars. Neither is a basic education enough for the employer. At least one college degree, if not a specialized secondary degree in a related field, is now required for most competitive entry-level positions.

What this means is that it isn't enough these days to make enough money to raise a family; it has become necessary to add to that astonishing financial responsibility the expenses associated with college for every child, or the equivalent (per child) of financing another household.

All of that still doesn't take into account the increase in the standard of living that typifies contemporary culture, the accruing of a respectable retirement, being able to afford the best available medical treatment, and the ability to leave a sizable estate for the children left behind.

It is very difficult, considering all of that, to keep one's perspective on money. The pressure to perform and accumulate is great, from within and without. Considering that fact, it is more and more difficult for the common individual to take to heart these words of Jesus: No one can serve two masters. Either he will hate the one and love the other, or he will be devoted to the one and despise the other. You cannot serve both God and Money (Matthew 6:24).

The truth is that many Christians are trying very hard to serve God and money. Perhaps most are straddling that fence. And there is very little exposure to a biblical perspective on finances available to your child, outside of your teaching and example. The instruction begins, obviously, with your commitment to Jesus' perspective on money and material goods. Listen to what He said.

> **Do not store up for yourselves treasures on earth, where moth and rust destroy, and where thieves break in and steal. But store up for yourselves treasures in heaven, where moth and rust do not destroy, and where thieves do not break in and steal. For where your treasure is, there your heart will be also.**
>
> **MATTHEW 6:19-21**

Money is an instrument that can buy you everything but happiness and pay your fare to every place but heaven.

Here are some suggestions with which to begin teaching:

Put the kingdom of God first.

"Mom," Chase panted, running down the stairs and into the kitchen. "I just heard on the radio that there is gonna be a drawing at the video game store at the mall at ten sharp tomorrow morning. They are giving away a new system and three games of your choice."

"Do you want me to swing by there on the way to church so you can put your name in the hat?"

"No! You have to be present to win."

"Oh, I see."

"Mom, you've got to understand. I can't go to church tomorrow. I'd be throwing away my chance to win."

"Chase, you're not throwing away anything by going to church tomorrow. You are, in fact, investing in your future."

One of the most challenging things parents face is teaching their children the principle of seeking spiritual priorities over material priorities. This just doesn't make much sense to a youngster who prefers to live for immediate gratification and the thrill of constant entertainment.

How does a parent fulfill this daunting task? By living daily in step with this kingdom principle joyfully and faithfully. Even though you can expect that your children will go head-to-head with you from time to time, they will be learning a lifestyle that will hold them accountable as adults, whether they like it or not!

Seeking first the kingdom means evaluating these financial issues:

★ What is the right occupation?

★ How much time and energy should be devoted to work?

★ Should advancement be pursued if more time and energy are required?

★ Is there such a thing as making too much money?

Live within your means.

From the time they are very young, you may teach your children the power of earning. Using an earned allowance, they can discover what it is to exchange the resource of work for the resource of money. Once that is accomplished, you have a perfect opportunity to further instruct them concerning tithing, saving, and spending. Children need to learn what it is to give to God first, save second, and spend last. Saving for something that they desire to purchase is a valuable experience. Many parents make the mistake of allowing their kids to make purchases prior to saving, teaching them, therefore, the dangerous seduction of debt—buy now, pay later.

Children need to learn what it is to give to God first, save second, and spend last.

If you teach them, on the other hand, the virtue of waiting, they learn two valuable lessons: patient endurance and living within their means. In addition, the anticipation is so sweet, it only increases the value of the item purchased. Your kids will be much prouder of their hard-earned possessions if they have worked and saved for the privilege of ownership. In fact, they will also learn a serendipitous respect for the possessions of others.

Live beneath your means, in order to live generously.

"Honey," the young man approached his wife at church in a whisper. "I just heard that Rose doesn't have enough money for groceries this week."

"Oh?" His wife's face melted with compassion as she glanced over her shoulder to see the woman to whom he was referring.

Rose was very poor, had three children—and she was single at the time. Recently, illness had caused her to miss a week of work.

"Daddy," Samantha felt compelled to enter into the discussion. "We barely have enough for our own food." At the ripe old age of eight, she had heard her mother tell her repeatedly at the grocery store that there wasn't money for the things she longed to buy.

"Sh-h-h," the young father frowned gently at Samantha. "We have more than enough." Turning back to his wife, he said: "I'm going to write her a $50 check."

The eyes of the young wife and mother widened involuntarily. That was twice the amount she spent on groceries every week. Still she answered, "You go ahead, Jim. The Lord will bless us for taking care of those in need."

The lesson wasn't lost on Samantha. She grew into a successful young woman with deep pockets and a deeper heart, always looking for those who needed what she could afford to give. Samantha never forgot the faith and generosity of her parents and, as a result, spent her life storing up treasure in heaven.

Children learn a great lesson about faith and character when they are taught to give beyond meager charitable offerings—to give from their hearts, to give until it hurts—and only then will they grasp the most significant blessing of earning money.

Teach your children to seek God first and take care of His concerns as a top priority, to live simply and unselfishly, and to give lavishly and joyfully. This is true abundance in living!

Drawing the Line
Teaching Your Kids How to Set Healthy Boundaries in Life

In the physical realm, boundaries are easily identified. There are walls around the house, a fence around the prison, the sidelines around a sporting field, the sidewalk around the lawn, and a shoreline around the water, etc. Teaching your children to respect these physical boundaries provides a foundation for living safely within community.

"Stay in our yard," the young mother reminds her son before he bolts out the door.

"I will, Mom," he shouts back over his shoulder. The fact is, Michael has learned that he can shinny up a tree that sits on the back corner of their lot and lean over the fence to talk to the "wayward" boy his mother is trying to protect him from.

Physical boundaries, though well-defined, are not always successful in their attempts at defining property, or in keeping people safe by hemming others in or out of their parameters. But physical boundaries are more easily enforced than those that are intangible. Laws regulating the violation of physical boundaries help protect society from chaos and violence.

The concept of boundaries in a personal and psychological dimension is much more difficult to explain to a child. The parameters of one's person are not comprised simply of the body that one inhabits—that would make it simple. However difficult, personal boundaries are important for children to understand in order to manage theirs responsibly.

"You can't tell me what to do," said the defiant little boy to his mother. "I'm God's property."

"You may be God's property," the mother responded, "but you're my responsibility."

Difficulty #1: Defining Boundaries

How does a parent explain personal boundaries to a child? First, the child should have a clear understanding that his body lies within his boundaries. Any behavior that anyone imposes upon a child that violates his psychological, emotional, or physical well-being by actions committed against his body should be clearly prohibited. For instance, the child needs to be taught the difference in being touched by a stranger as opposed to a family member or close friend.

Moreover, in today's unsafe world, a child needs to be taught what is acceptable "touch" even within the family or close friendships. Though you don't want to alarm your children to the extent that they hold everyone suspect, you do need to establish a clear understanding of what is permissible, what is not, and what to do if something impermissible occurs.

In today's unsafe world, a child needs to be taught what is acceptable "touch" even within the family or close friendships.

Second, and more difficult to convey, is the idea that invisible parts of a person—those that come from within—lie within their boundaries, as well. That would include:

- ★ Emotions
- ★ Beliefs /values
- ★ Thoughts /attitudes
- ★ Actions /behavior
- ★ Words
- ★ Talents /abilities
- ★ Desires /needs

Once children begin to understand that their "person" encompasses attributes that are not perceivable with the eyes, then they can grasp the boundaries associated with them.

Third, there are those things within your child's boundaries that incorporate outside individuals, activities, or entities.

- ★ Relationships
- ★ Responsibilities
- ★ Commitments

These aspects of one's "person" are intricately intertwined with other persons. The benefit of defining boundaries to this extent will help your children understand what they are responsible for, as well as what they aren't.

"Mom, I have to go to Mindy's house Friday night or she'll just fall apart."

"Honey," her mom answered, "you are responsible to Mindy, but you are not responsible for Mindy."

There is a difference in taking responsibility for her treatment of another individual and taking responsibility for the individual altogether.

Difficulty #2: Establishing Boundaries

Teaching your children the parameters of their existence will help them develop in at least two ways:

1. They will develop a healthy sense of responsibility for their own personal well-being and take the necessary actions to ensure that they are safe and comfortable.

2. They will develop a healthy respect for the boundaries of others, ensuring their self-discipline in relationships and their participation in the safety and well-being of others.

The objective is to understand one's individuality as separate from others yet have a good grasp of the interdependence that exists among a community of loving individuals.

"I am whole, yet I am a part of a bigger whole."

Difficulty #3: Managing Boundaries

Teach your children that their personal boundaries should be managed with clear communication: saying what you expect and expecting what you say. A clear and distinct yes should indicate that the child wishes to participate within the parameters defined. A clear and distinct no should indicate that the child does not wish to participate, and any coercion or manipulation should be interpreted as a violation of his parameters.

A third-grader showed up at a classmate's house with a baseball bat. His intentions were not to initiate a sandlot baseball game, but to hit his classmate with the bat. He rapped loudly on the front door of his classmate's house. Having been apprised of the boy's intentions, the classmate's older and much larger brother answered the door: "Can I help you?"

"Can I talk to Ben?" the boy asked angrily.

"No," Ben's brother answered.

The boy didn't budge off the porch.

"What else can I help you with?" Ben's older brother probed.

"I'm not leaving till Ben comes out here."

"Oh, you're leaving all right," the broad-shouldered sibling announced. "Ben doesn't want to talk to you while you're holding a baseball bat, so you can leave here cooperatively with your bat, or you can leave here with a pile of splinters. Your choice." Ben's brother stepped out the door and onto the porch, towering over the third-grader.

"Okay, I'm leaving." The boy paled.

"Then take steps," Ben's brother finished, standing akimbo until the little bully was beyond the boundaries of Ben's yard.

123

Difficulty #4: Respecting Boundaries

"She hit me!" three-year-old Sheila yelled from the living room.

"She hit me first!" her sister screamed louder.

The twins' mom walked into the room and looked at the two girls, shaking her head. Wisely, she instructed them: "Each of you can touch the other's skin only in loving ways. Any kind of touch that isn't loving isn't allowed."

All children have a vague understanding of boundaries. Likewise, all children need some instruction about how to respect boundaries—theirs and others.

All children have a vague understanding of boundaries. Likewise, all children need some instruction about how to respect boundaries—theirs and others.

[Jesus said,] "Always do for other people everything you want them to do for you."

MATTHEW 7:12 GOD'S WORD

If it were going to be easy to raise kids,
it wouldn't have started with
something called "labor."

Anonymous

Parenting Pitfalls

Let us therefore no longer pass judgment on one another,
but resolve instead never to put a stumbling block or hindrance
in the way of another.

ROMANS 14:13 NRSV

"I Can't Let You Out of My Sight."
Overprotectiveness

"Rachel, please don't argue with me. I said no!"

"But, Mom, for heaven's sake. It's not a spring break trip. It's a mission trip, and I'm 17 years old."

"I'm just not comfortable with your going," Rachel's mom stated again. "It's Mexico—anything could happen."

"Mom, it's perfectly safe. We'll be in a group, working on a church project. There will be eight adults—and I'm not in first grade. Don't you trust me at all?" Rachel asked, her voice beginning to rise in pitch and shudder with frustration and anger. "I've never given you any reason not to trust me. It's completely unfair."

"I'm just thinking about all the things that could happen down there. I'm just trying to keep you safe."

"I don't know why I'm surprised, Mom," Rachel said before slamming the door to her room. "You never let me do anything."

The solution to Rachel's predicament is probably obvious to you as you read this story, but a tendency to be overly protective is often less easy to spot when it involves you and your child.

It isn't easy being a parent, trying to second-guess every situation and evaluate the dangers based on little or no evidence. But to some extent, godly parents must trust God to keep their children safe. Let fear get the best of you, hold on too tight, and you are apt to drive a wedge between you and your child and impede his or her spiritual growth. Certainly there is a need for common sense, but the best outcome is the result of balancing physical risk with spiritual and emotional benefits. Let God help you sidestep overprotectiveness and allow your child to grow and mature.

"I'm Exhausted—You're Exhausted."
Extreme Busyness

Janice looked up from her desk at her 12-year-old son.

"Can't this wait, honey? I'm trying to finish up some work of my own."

"But I've got to do this tonight, Mom! The test is tomorrow," said Brian, an edge of desperation creeping into his voice. "I've already studied all the chapters. I just need you to quiz me on the chapter reviews."

Janice shoved the papers away from her wearily. She'd been looking forward to a little time to herself that evening. A chance to unwind from her long day at the office, maybe even start that novel she'd picked up the week before—or was it two weeks ago?

She sighed inwardly, trying to hide her irritation. She was running out of steam, and her son's needs were draining her even further.

Being a parent is a full-time job in itself. Add in the stress of a career, and the normal demands of life, and you've got a recipe for exhaustion. And single parents can multiply that equation exponentially. They really are doing the work of two people.

So what's the solution? How do you avoid the burnout that can so easily overtake you as a parent? First, take care of your own physical needs. There were times, in the Bible, when God told someone to just go to sleep. He knew that to have the energy to be your best requires rest. And second, godly parenting requires that you take a good look at your priorities. Are you spending your time—and energy—on things that exhaust you? And if so, how is that affecting your children?

Ask God for wisdom to cut out the unnecessary things in your life that may be draining you of the energy you need to be your best. And then trust Him for good rest and renewed energy for each new day.

"What I Need You to Be."
Exaggerated Expectations

Katherine threw up her hands in frustration.

"I'm doing the best I can, Mom!" she practically yelled. "All my friends are failing this class, and I'm getting a B. What more do you want from me?"

Her mom paced the floor. "You know you have to get all A's to get that scholarship, don't you? Even one B can ruin your chances."

Tears sprang to Katherine's eyes. "But I'm studying hours every night for this one class—I don't even have a social life anymore!" She swiped angrily at her face. "You're ruining my life, Mom!"

Katherine turned and stormed from the room.

We all have expectations for our kids, don't we? So many hopes and dreams for their future. And many of them depend on their doing well—at school, at sports, on the stage. But how do we know when we've crossed the line that separates realistic expectations from exaggerated expectations? When is "just enough" not good enough?

It's natural to want our kids to succeed. God wants that for His children too. But we must be careful not to measure their success by the wrong standards. Godly parenting involves evaluating our motives and making sure that our expectations are really about what's best for our child. Perhaps it is important for them to maintain good grades to get a scholarship; but do they have to be class valedictorian as well? Could it be that some of the expectations we place on our kids are really a reflection of our own unfulfilled dreams and goals?

Perhaps we need to allow our kids a little more room to fail—a chance to make a mistake or two.

Relaxing your expectations may actually help motivate your children to set their own goals for their lives, rather than relying on yours. And then, when they've met those goals, it'll be a victory you both can be proud of.

"I Know Who You Are."
Labeling Your Child

Dan watched his son grab his skateboard from the hall closet. Joe yelled as he ran out the door, "I'll be home for dinner!"

Dan's eyebrows flew up as the front door slammed shut. He looked over at his wife, Susan.

"That's the third time this week he's gone skateboarding with those guys," he said. Susan nodded distractedly from behind her book.

"Don't you worry that he's turning into one of those kids who doesn't do anything but hang out with their loser buddies all day, and then come home and watch hours of TV every night?" he persisted.

Susan put down her book. "You can't assume bad things are in store for our son just because he's at the skate park a lot."

Dan shook his head and reached for his paper. "I can guarantee you this, Susan: If Joe doesn't get some new friends, and start being more responsible, he's never going to amount to anything!"

It's easy to label children. We see the studious ones, carrying their pocket protectors and wearing their glasses, and immediately label them nerds (or envision them as the next Bill Gates). And we're quick to pigeonhole the artsy theater types, who wear flamboyant clothes and speak in French; or the ones who smell like smoke and disappear, mysteriously, every afternoon.

It's easy to label them—but should we? Perhaps God wants us to see beyond what's visible, to the heart underneath that ripped T-shirt. Too often, we judge a child by his outward appearance; but God knows what's really going on in our kids' hearts.

So let's work to not label our children so quickly. As godly parents, let's speak good things—blessings—over them. Let's believe that, no matter what preconceived notions we might have about the "type" of children they are, each one is a precious, unique individual in God's eyes. And He's got great plans in store for each one of them!

"Let Me Get That for You."
Helping Too Much

Katrina's mom studied the flowers laid out carefully on the dining room table. "If you glued the pink ones on the blue paper, that would look nice."

Katrina sighed. "Mom, I can do this. It's my science project, remember?"

Her mom reached for a book. "At least let me help you press them—"

Katrina stopped her, midsentence. "I can do it! Don't you have some other stuff you've got to do?"

Her mom dropped the book on the table, irritated. "I was just trying to help, Katrina. You do what you want!"

She left, banging the door as she went.

Katrina buried her head in her hands. Why did her mom always try to barge in? It'd gotten to the point where she didn't even want to tell her when she had a school project due anymore. Might as well label it "Made by Katrina and her mom," she thought glumly.

Are you sometimes guilty of this—"helping" your child a little too much? We probably all are. It's natural to want to come to their rescue when they're facing a challenging homework assignment or learning a new skill. But when does helping them cross over into hurting them?

It's true that God wants us to teach our children the right way to do things. To guide them, so they can learn to make wise choices. But at some point we've got to release them and let them make their own decisions.

Godly parents can rest in the assurance that, when we teach our kids to make good choices, they'll be more likely to do the right thing when they're older. Those lessons learned while they're young will stay in their hearts as they grow.

So the next time you're tempted to "help," ask yourself if this might be one time when your child would do better without your assistance. Step back a bit; and then watch good things happen!

"Why Can't You Be Like Him?"
Making Comparisons

Brian threw his test down on the counter.

"It's hopeless," he sighed. "I'll never get better than a C in chemistry."

His father looked up at this. "A C? I thought you studied for this one."

"I did, Dad—I spent hours going over it."

"But, Brian," his dad said frowning, "Philip aced that same test last year."

Brian felt the anger rising inside him. Why did his parents always have to compare him to his older—and smarter—brother? Everything came so easy for Philip. It wasn't fair. And the worst part was, even Brian's teachers expected a lot from him because he was related to Philip.

"Philip's a genius, okay, Dad?" Brian said through clenched teeth. "Guess I'm just the family idiot!"

He stormed from the room.

Brian's dad picked up the test, his heart heavy. He didn't mean to compare his two sons—but it was hard not to. Everything did seem to come easier for Philip. And Brian? Well, he always seemed a few paces behind.

Perhaps you can relate to Brian's dad. One of your kids has a special talent in an area—and the other one doesn't. It's natural to want your children to excel, and to nurture their abilities. But do you sometimes encourage one child to the detriment of the other?

If every child is made in God's image, and God has a plan for each one, then it's up to us, as godly parents, to help them discover their individual abilities. Maybe your child is good at something that you never were—and so it's harder to understand their enthusiasm for certain subjects or activities. But you can still encourage the development of that talent and praise your child for his or her own special abilities.

No one likes to be compared to someone else. So let's work to recognize—and encourage—the marvelous qualities that make each of our children unique.

"I Had Every Intention . . . "
Breaking Promises

Tom called home from the airport.

"Looks like my flight's been delayed," he said. "I won't make it home until tomorrow night."

"But you promised the kids we'd go to the beach tomorrow!" his wife, Janice, said. "They've been looking forward to it all week."

Tom's voice rose in irritation. "Look, Janice, I can't help it if I'm stuck here. What am I supposed to do? Flag down a jet on the runway?"

Janice suppressed a smart remark. *It won't help to get mad at him,* she thought. Still, she couldn't help feeling frustrated. Too many times lately Tom had promised the kids they'd go on a special outing—only to disappoint them at the last minute. And now she'd have to break the bad news to them and bear the brunt of their anger.

How many times are we guilty of breaking a promise to our children? We smile broadly and talk about the great time we'll have at the park, at the movies, when we go to that restaurant— and then something comes up. Suddenly, that promise gets shoved aside as something more urgent takes center stage.

As godly parents, we need to be aware of how vital it is to keep our promises. It conveys to our children how important they are to us. Broken promises lead to distrust and the sneaking suspicion that other things are really more important to us.

Perhaps we need to pause a moment before making promises—especially if we're not sure we can keep them. Even though we're promising less, we're following through more, allowing our children to relax and begin to trust us. And then, when those rare emergencies do come up when we aren't able to follow through, our children will be more apt to understand.

"Don't Worry About Me—Really."
Motivating With Guilt

Tammy looked at the mound of dishes piled high in the sink. Her mood sank as she contemplated the dinner still left to make, the kids' homework to oversee.

Her son came in and grabbed a cookie. "What time's dinner, Mom?"

Tammy sighed. "Whenever I can get to it. I've got so much cleaning up to do."

Her son reached for his ball glove. "Okay if I go throw a few balls?"

Tammy nodded slowly. "I guess."

Her son stopped in the doorway, looking back at her. His face betrayed his conflicting emotions.

"Do you want me to stay and help, or something?"

Tammy shook her head. "No, I'll be fine—really. You go ahead."

Her son cast a guilty look back at his mom as he headed out the door. Somehow, his steps seemed a little less carefree.

Guilt can really be used as a weapon, can't it? We want something from our children; but rather than coming out and saying it, we use subterfuge to get what we want. The problem is that our kids get mixed messages when we use this technique. On the one hand, we say we really don't want something; but our actions or facial expressions say otherwise. It can confuse kids and make them unsure of our expectations.

As godly parents, it's so important to be up front with our children. When we talk with them openly about our expectations, it communicates that we respect them. It also helps build their confidence because our expectations are clearly laid out and they know there's no danger of "missing" our cues.

So the next time you're tempted to use guilt to get something, stop yourself! Try a little open communication instead. You'll likely find yourself rejoicing that your children have helped you willingly—and without all that guilt.

"Don't Make Me Come in There."
Threatening Words

Karen cocked an ear toward her girls' bedroom. Once again, it sounded as if they were quarreling over something. She sighed and dragged herself from the couch, her irritation growing with every step.

"What are you two fighting over now?" she asked through the closed bedroom door.

Her daughter Ashley opened it a crack. "Mom, Jenny keeps hogging the computer! She's been on there for almost an hour."

Karen pushed past her, angry now. Her other daughter wheeled around.

"That's not true!" wailed Jenny. "I've only been on for 20 minutes. Besides, I promised I'd help my friend with—"

Karen cut her off, her voice rising. "Jenny, I don't want to hear another word! Let your sister on there right this instant!"

Jenny's face crumpled. "But, Mom—"

"Don't 'but Mom' me! If you're not off there in 30 seconds, you'll be grounded from the computer for the rest of the month!"

Karen turned and slammed the door shut. There—matter settled.

So why did she suddenly feel so out of control?

We've probably all had times when we've resorted to threats with our kids. We're tired, the day's been a long one, and we frankly don't have the patience to listen to long explanations. So we issue an ultimatum and then leave, hoping they'll learn from the experience. Unfortunately, what our kids often learn is that threatening is a good way to cope with conflict.

As godly parents, we need to stop and catch ourselves before we speak, before those threats come pouring from our lips. If our desire is to grow closer to our children, we need to control our words.

Look to God for help in this area. He's promised that if we take the time to listen to our kids and work to find a solution, they'll learn things that will help them as they deal with future conflicts in their own lives.

"You Missed a Little Over Here."
Micromanagement

Randy threw down his rag in disgust.

"So I missed a few spots on the car, Dad—what's the big deal?"

His father, Ken, pointed to a big smear on the body of the shiny SUV. "It's more than a few spots, Randy. See this?"

Randy shrugged. "No one's going to notice that, Dad. Besides, can't we take a break? We've been waxing the car for almost an hour!"

Ken shook his head. "It's not good to leave a job half finished, Randy. Don't you want to feel proud of your work?"

Randy turned away, muttering something under his breath. Halfheartedly, he picked up the rag again.

Ken frowned and sat back on his heels, discouraged. This was supposed to be a father-and-son thing, a time to grow closer.

So, why was everything going so wrong?

You might be able to spot the problem in this scene right away. Ken seems to have fallen into the common trap of micro-managing his son's work. And it's leading Randy to feel resentful—and rightfully so.

It's easy, as parents, to want our kids to do everything perfectly. We want them to take pride in their work, and that's usually a good thing. But when we go overboard and insist on perfection, we can find ourselves unhappy and our children frustrated.

Godly parenting requires us to know when to say, "That's good enough," and to be pleased when our children make an effort—even if it's not perfect. Allow them the freedom to experiment, to try new things. If you're supportive of their efforts, they're likely to step out even further next time. Trust them to do the best job they can. And then, when they do a job well, your praise will mean that much more to them.

"See No Evil."
Refusing to Face Your Child's Faults and Failings

John shifted in his chair, uncomfortable under the watchful gaze of his daughter's teacher, Mrs. Myers. She did not look pleased.

"You do realize," she continued, "that Alison has also been bullying several of her classmates?"

John raised his hands in the air defensively. "Now, hold on there, Mrs. Myers. I wouldn't call a little good-natured kidding 'bullying'!"

Mrs. Myers frowned. "She's been calling other kids 'losers' and slamming their locker doors on their fingers."

"I'm sure Ali didn't mean to hurt them," John protested. "Have you ever considered that these other kids might just be a little overly sensitive?"

He stood to leave.

"But don't worry," he said. "I'll be sure to ask her about it. It was probably all just a big misunderstanding."

John turned and left.

Mrs. Myers sat back and sighed heavily. She knew he'd never talk to his daughter.

Unfortunately, Alison's teacher was probably right. Once we're in the habit of making excuses for our children, it's hard to honestly confront their faults and failings.

It's difficult to admit that they might be struggling in certain areas. We like to think that they're perfect (though, deep down, most of us realize that they're really not).

Part of being a godly parent means having the willingness to look at our children with a critical eye. Not criticizing them, but evaluating their characters—the good and the bad points. And being honest with ourselves: Have we allowed unacceptable behavior to continue because we don't want to confront them? Only when we're ruthlessly honest will we be able to help our children improve in areas where they're weak. Although this evaluation may be difficult, in the long run, it'll really pay off.

"Don't Worry—I'll Get You Out of This." Codependency

Cindy leaned over the table, next to her son Craig, and studied the map laid out in front of him. "So, you've got to glue the red flags on all the Communist countries?"

He nodded, his face screwed up in frustration. "Mom, I'm never going to finish this project by tomorrow! And I've got soccer practice this afternoon."

"It's due tomorrow? But it's Sunday. Why didn't you work on it yesterday when you had more time?"

He shrugged. "I dunno. I just forgot about it."

He grabbed her arm intently.

"Can you help me work on this, Mom? I bet we could finish it up in an hour or two!"

Cindy sighed inwardly. She'd hoped to do some yard work this afternoon. And then there was the laundry, and those phone calls to make for church.

But she suppressed her irritation, pulled up a chair, and sat down.

"Hand me a flag," she said, reaching for the glue.

Are we guilty of doing what Cindy is doing—helping our children out a little too much? If we're always rescuing them when they're in trouble, how will they ever learn from their mistakes? Perhaps, in trying to help so much, we're really doing them a disservice.

We'll probably always battle our desires to help our children, even as we strive to be godly parents. After all, God created us with an inborn desire to protect them and help them. But if we step back from time to time and let them fall out of the nest, we're really enabling them, in a positive way, to grow—independent of our help.

So let's step aside and allow our children to fail occasionally. The experience will only strengthen them and help them develop the willpower to stick with a project and see it to completion. To develop perseverance so that one day they can grow into responsible adults.

"You Push All My Buttons."
Anger

Jill stood back and surveyed her daughter's room with satisfaction. After hours of work, the redecorating was done. Baby blue walls enveloped the room; a fluffy white comforter and lace shams nestled on the bed.

As her daughter slammed the front door, Jill smiled in anticipation. She'd done all the redecorating while her daughter was at school—and it was all a surprise.

But when her daughter stopped dead outside the bedroom door and stared at her room in horror, Jill felt anger start to rise up in her.

"Mom, that's not the color I wanted my room painted!" her daughter wailed. "We agreed on neon green!"

"But blue is such a soothing color."

"I don't want 'soothing', Mom, I want 'hot'! And this is all so . . . little girly!"

Jill clenched her fists tightly, seething inside. She was tempted to throw the wet paintbrush at her daughter. *I never had such a nice room when I was a kid*, she thought.

Our kids can push our buttons sometimes, can't they? And often, it seems the oddest things can make us angry. It's as if our children have internal radar that can zoom in on our most sensitive areas.

One of the challenges of being a godly parent is being willing to honestly evaluate these areas in our own lives. Anger is a normal human reaction. But if we become unusually angry in certain situations, it might be a clue that there are unresolved issues that need to be dealt with.

Being honest about our own shortcomings, and then allowing God to heal us in those areas, can be keys to overcoming excessive anger toward our children. And then, the next time one of our children pushes our buttons, we'll be able to deal with the situation more rationally and help bring about a satisfying resolution—without throwing any paintbrushes his or her way!

"I Asked You to Do It This Way."
Trying to Control

Jeff threw up his hands in frustration. "I don't get it, Mom. What does it matter if the light-colored clothes go in the same pile as the whites?"

Jody peered at her son over the mound of dirty laundry. "I've already told you, Jeff! Different colors take different temperatures of water."

Jeff began heaving clothes into the washer. "What's the big deal, anyway? Half the guys in my dorm don't even do their own laundry—they just take it home."

"It's important that you learn to do it right," Jody said, her voice firm.

Inside, though, a little doubt had begun to creep into Jody. *Why is it so important that he do this perfectly? It's only laundry, after all.*

Perhaps your children are nearing the age when they'll strike out on their own, and you're suddenly seized with panic, wondering how in the world they'll cope. You mentally review all the things you neglected to teach them and determine to teach them everything you know in the next few months. But then, if they don't do things exactly like you want them to, you find yourself getting upset.

It's common for parents to want things done just so. Could it be that we're trying to control our children out of fear that they'll never learn on their own, that they'll grow up to be irresponsible and lazy?

God can help us release our anxieties, if we ask Him to. Godly parenting sometimes means we release our death grip on the steering wheel of our children's lives and trust that God will take care of them and teach them what they need to know.

So take a deep breath, relax, and let your children learn and grow through their mistakes and mishaps. After all, a few pink-colored undershirts never hurt anybody!

Good parents give their children roots and wings.
Roots to know where home is,
wings to fly away and exercise
what's been taught them.

Jonas Salk

Gems for Your Journey

Choose for yourselves this day whom you will
serve. . . . But as for me and my household,
we will serve the Lord.

JOSHUA 24:15

Inspiration & Motivation for the Road Ahead

There is just one way to bring up a child in the way he should go and that is to travel that way yourself.

Abraham Lincoln

Kids are not a short-term loan,
they are a long-term investment.

James Dobson

Those children who are of sufficient years to sin and be saved by faith have to listen to the gospel and receive it by faith. And they can do this, God the Holy Spirit helping them. There is no doubt about it, because great numbers have done it. I will not say at what age children are first capable of receiving the knowledge of Christ, but it is much earlier than some fancy.

C. H. Spurgeon

Lying can never save us from another lie.

Václav Havel

I will act as if what I do makes a difference.

William James

Life's most persistent and urgent question is,
"What are you doing for others?"

Martin Luther King Jr.

No one is useless in this world who
lightens the burdens of another.

Charles Dickens

It's nice to be important, but it is more important to be nice.
John Marks

Don't judge each day by the harvest you reap,
but by the seeds you plant.
Robert Louis Stevenson

Hang around doggies and kids; they know how to play.
Geoffrey Godbey

Children have never been very good at listening to their
elders, but they have never failed to imitate them.
James Baldwin

Enjoy the little things in life, for one day you will look back
and realize they were the big things.
Anonymous

It is because we are different that each of us is special.
Brian Dyson

Children in a family are like flowers in a bouquet:
there's always one determined to face in an opposite
direction from the way the arranger desires.
Marcelene Cox

For the mother is and must be, whether she knows it or not,
the greatest, strongest, and most lasting teacher
her children have.
Hannah Whitall Smith

Try This!
Family Traditions

Family Altar

The family altar was once a constant in homes across the country—a tradition that is happily making a comeback. Families meet not one, not two, but five nights a week for family devotions and prayer.

In our high-fidelity, rocket-fast society, such an idea might seem laughable. But it can work and might even serve as an incentive to assess priorities and trim back overbooked schedules. At any rate, family altar need not displace family life as you now know it.

A short devotional and prayer as a family at breakfast or before bed at night is a realistic goal. It might be met with some protests at first, but most kids—even in the teen years—will soon learn to accept and even enjoy the time. A short relevant devotional is best, with a moderate challenge at the end. Switch it up with a lot of different authors. Then pray for your family, asking God's hand of protection and blessing as the day unfolds. Long after they're grown, your children will remember that you put God first in your home.

Bless Me's

When you tuck your child in at night, ask the child to repeat his or her bless me's. They follow like this:

Bless my daddy.

Bless my mommy.

Bless my brother/sister, [sibling's name].

Bless my grandmother/grandfather, [name].

Bless my teacher, [name].

Bless my friend, [name].

Bless my neighbor, [name].

Bless my cousin, [name].

Continue until your child has covered every member of the family (immediate and extended) and all those in his or her world. Don't forget the pets.

This tradition has a number of benefits:

★ It enhances the sense that God cares about the child and the child's loved ones, personally as well as corporately—God calls us by name.

★ It instills a sense of family ties—God has set us in families.

★ It reinforces the feeling that we are to look after one another—God has commanded us to love and care for one another.

★ It quiets the child for sleep.

★ It establishes a habit of communing with God before sleep each night.

Hands Around the Table

Prayer before meals is enhanced when the family holds hands around the table. Include even the baby in the high chair. As soon as the food has been passed, begin with the oldest child and ask each to express a blessing received that day.

When grace is given, add this to be spoken by everyone in union:

Thank you for the food we are about to eat
and for the blessings we have this day received.
Amen.

Prayers to Pray
Praying for Your Kids—Examples

Parents often have trouble when it comes to praying for their kids. It's just so easy to let your own desires and aspirations come to the surface. So how can you be certain that you are praying properly—within the will of God? The best way is by praying the Scriptures over your children.

A Prayer for My Child's Salvation Based on Ephesians 3:17-19:

Heavenly Father:
I pray that Christ would dwell in [child's name] heart by faith; that [he/she], being rooted and grounded in love, may be able to understand Him better and know His love, which passes all knowledge. I pray that [child's name] might be filled with all the fullness of God.
Amen.

A Prayer for My Child to Grow in Love for God's Word Based on Psalm 1:2-3:

Heavenly Father:
I pray that [child's name] will delight in your Word and meditate on it day and night, so that [he/she] will be like a tree planted by the rivers of water that brings forth fruit in its season. I pray that the result will be that [child's name] will prosper in whatever [he/she] does.
Amen.

A Prayer for My Child for Wisdom and Discernment Based on James 1:5-6:

Heavenly Father:
I pray for [child's name] to receive your wisdom. Thank you for
giving it liberally. I ask for the faith as well—faith to ask and
receive without wavering. And I ask that this wisdom would
lead to good choices and right paths for [child's name].
Amen.

A Prayer for My Child When He or She Needs Discipline Based on Proverbs 29:17:

Heavenly Father:
I pray that you would help me to discipline [child's name] in
ways that are pleasing to you. With the administering of that
discipline, I pray that [child's name] would receive your peace
and bring delight to your heart and mine.
Amen.

A Prayer for My Child When He or She Needs Comfort Based on Psalm 34:18:

Heavenly Father:
My child, [child's name], is brokenhearted. I pray that you will
be close by during this time of need. Make your presence
apparent in both [his/her] heart and mind. And I pray that you
would touch and heal [his/her] crushed spirit.
Amen.

A Prayer for My Child Regarding His or Her Future Based on Jeremiah 29:11:

Heavenly Father:
I know you have a plan and a purpose for [child's name]. It is a plan to prosper [him/her] and not for harm. Thank you for giving [child's name] a hope and a future.
Amen.

A Prayer for My Child When He or She Needs Joy Based on Psalm 16:11:

Heavenly Father:
I pray that you would make known to [child's name] the path of life. I pray that you will fill [him/her] with joy in your presence and with eternal pleasures at your right hand.
Amen.

A Prayer for My Child When He or She Needs an Attitude of Obedience Based on Deuteronomy 13:4:

Heavenly Father:
I pray that [child's name] would follow you, revere you, keep your commands and obey you, serve you, and hold fast to you. When [child's name] has learned to obey and revere you, I know that [he/she] will also obey and revere me.
Amen.

A Prayer for My Child When He or She Needs Self-Worth Based on Matthew 10:29-31:

Heavenly Father:
Your Word says that you care for the lowly little sparrows. You know each time even one of these little creatures falls to the ground and dies. I pray that you would help [child's name] to realize that you value [him/her] much more than you value the lowly sparrow. Impress on [him/her] that you care about even the smallest details—even the number of hairs on [his/her] head. Then help [him/her] to realize that [he/she] must also value [himself/herself].
Amen.

149

A Prayer for My Child When He or She Needs Strength Based on 2 Samuel 22:33-34:

Heavenly Father:
I pray that you will arm [child's name] with strength and make [his/her] way perfect. I pray that you would make [child's name] feet like the feet of a deer and enable [him/her] to stand on the heights of success.
Amen.

A Prayer for My Child When He or She Has Strayed from the Lord Based on Ezekiel 34:16:

Heavenly Father:
I pray that you would search for my lost child [child's name] and bring [him/her] back to us and to you. Bind up [his/her] injuries and strengthen [his/her] weaknesses.
Amen.

Prayers to Share
Praying With Your Kids—Examples

Though you will want to engage your children with prayers appropriate for their ages, these easy-to-memorize prayers teach the proper components and attitudes of heartfelt communication with God, while being good models for more spontaneous communication as your children grow.

Thank You, Lord

Thank you for the world so sweet;
Thank you for the food we eat;
Thank you for the birds that sing;
Thank you, God, for ev'rything.
Amen.

-E. Rutter Leatham

A Child's Prayer for Morning

My God, I offer to you this day
all I think or do or say,
in union with all you've done for me
by Jesus Christ your Son.
Dear Lord, I rise from bed to pray;
then soon go out to school or play.
Let all I meet along the way
see you in me throughout the day.
Amen.

I Give Today

O Jesus, I give you today,
all that I think and do and say.

O Jesus. I love you and pray
more love today than yesterday,
O God, be with me I pray;
be by my side forever to stay.
Amen.

Prayer before Meals.

Bless us, O Lord, and these your gifts, which we are about to
receive from your bounty through Christ our Lord.
Amen.

Nighttime Prayers
Now I Lay Me Down to Sleep

Now I lay me down to sleep,
I pray Thee, Lord, Thy child to keep:
Thy love guard me through the night
And wake me with the morning light.
Amen.

Time has come for me to sleep,
And I thank Thee for Thy keep.
Watch this night well over me;
Teach me, Lord, to trust in Thee.
Many sins I've done today;
Please, Lord, take them all away.
Look upon me in Thy grace,
Make me pure before Thy face.
Care for children sick and poor,
Grant them, Lord, Thy blessing more.
Care for Mom and Dad the same;
This I pray in Jesus' name.
Amen.

Bedtime Song

All praise to you, my God, this night,
for all the blessings of the light.
Keep me, O keep me, King of kings,
beneath the shelter of your wings.

Forgive me, Lord, for this I pray,
the wrong that I have done this day.
May peace with God and neighbor be,
before I sleep, restored to me.

Lord, may I be at rest in you
and sweetly sleep the whole night through.
Refresh my strength, for your own sake,
that I may serve you when I wake.

Praise God from Whom all blessings flow;
Praise Him all creatures here below.
Praise Him above, you heavenly host;
Praise Father, Son, and Holy Ghost.

Amen.

The House of the Lord
Tips for Finding a Local Church Home for Your Family

Finding a church home for your family is crucial for parents engaged in raising godly kids.

A church family provides for you, the parent:

- ★ Affirmation of concepts you are teaching in the home.

- ★ Support and encouragement when you are struggling with your child.

- ★ Additional resources for your task.

- ★ Opportunities for personal spiritual growth.

A church family provides for your child:

- ★ Reinforcement of concepts learned in the home.

- ★ A proving ground for the practice of godliness through conflict and conflict resolution in a godly environment.

- ★ Realization of the comfort and support needed to live a godly life.

- ★ A circle of Christian friends.

10 Tips for Finding a Church Home

1. Have a discussion with your family to find out what everyone is looking for in a church home.

2. Look for a church with a strong ministry to families, rather than just to children.

3. Choose a church that openly preaches and affirms the deity of Christ, His death and resurrection, and salvation only through Him.

4. Choose a church that shows signs of life and health—friendliness, enthusiasm, compassion, and outreach to its community.

5. Check out the pastor and the pastoral staff. Are they personable, accessible, and humble?

6. Look for a church with vibrant praise and worship. This does not necessarily mean bigger and more sophisticated, but rather the enthusiasm of the congregants.

7. Ask questions and expect an open and unambiguous explanation of beliefs.

8. Choose a church where the members treat each other like family.

9. Look for outreaches that will allow you and your children to serve the community.

10. Visit a number of churches at least once and your short list at least four times before committing to join one of them.

10 Questions to Ask After Visiting a Prospective Church:

1. Did you feel any tension among members?

2. Did the pastor seem aloof or detached from the congregants on a personal level?

3. Did the sermon and other teaching sessions refer the listener to the Bible and invite the congregants to read the Bible for themselves?

4. Were you and your family made to feel welcomed?

5. Did you feel pressured in any way?

6. Did you sense any of these traits in the pastor or the congregation: controlling, blaming, delusional, distrustful?

7. Were the children in the congregation—for the most part—respectful, happy, and under control?

8. Was the church an open book in terms of history and affiliations?

9. Was there an overemphasis on any one aspect of church life?

10. Did you feel peaceful, comfortable, and joyful as you sat in the congregation?

You wouldn't move into a home that you had not thoroughly checked out. You would make sure that it was big enough but not too big, accommodated your family size and preferences, and would provide the comfort and security your family needs. Why would you give less care to choosing a church home?

See several church locator Web sites listed in the next section.

A Way in the Wilderness

Resources for Growing Godly Kids—Web Sites, Books, Resources, Church Finders, Devotional Material for Kids, Child-Friendly Bible Translations

Helpful Web sites:

★ *forMINISTRY.com* (American Bible Society) allows you to search online among thousands of listings for a church home by inputting denomination, city, state, and zip code.

★ *NowtryGod.com* provides a church finder link that allows you to type in your zip code and see all the churches in the area.

★ *ABCBibleStudy.com* offers simple Bible studies on a variety of everyday topics.

★ *Graceandtruthbooks.com* specializes in character-building books for the family.

★ *Praymag.com* (Navigators) offers a bookmark prayer card titled "31 Biblical Virtues to Pray for Your Kids." One biblical character quality, along with a Scripture prayer, is listed for each day of the month.

★ *Gospelcom.net* features Keys for Kids (CBH Ministries), a bi-monthly devotional publication for kids and online daily Bible reading and devotional.

Books:

★ *Faith Training: Raising Kids Who Love the Lord* by Dr. Joe White. Time-tested ways to disciple your sons and daughters. Based on the model presented in Paul's letter to Timothy, he gives practical advice on how to "train up a child in the way he should go." Focus on the Family Publishing.

★ *Raising Great Kids* by Dr. Henry Cloud and Dr. John Townsend. How you can help your child develop six necessary character traits: attachment, responsibility, reality, competence, morality, and worship/spiritual life. Zondervan Publishing House.

Reader-Friendly Bible Translations:

★ *The Living Bible*, Reading Level: Grade 8.3
Using the *American Standard Version* as his working text, Kenneth Taylor rephrased the Bible into modern speech in 1962. His goal was to create a paraphrase that would allow anyone, even a child, to understand the message of the original writers.

★ *The Message*, Reading Level: Grade 8.5
The Message, published in 1993 by NavPress, is a free, highly colloquial and interpretive translation/paraphrase of the New Testament by Eugene H. Peterson.

★ *The New King James Version*, Reading Level: Grade 8.5
The New King James Version, published by Thomas Nelson Publishers in 1982, is a revision of the King James Version. It retains the elegant literary style of the KJV, but is easier to read.

★ *The New Living Translation*, Reading Level: Grade 6.3
The New Living Translation, published by Tyndale in 1996, is a "thorough revision" of The Living Bible.

★ *The New Century Version*, Reading Level: Grade 3
The International Children's Bible, New Century Version, published by Nelson Bibles in 2000, is said to be one of the easiest-to-read translations available.

Read Along
A Kid's Guide to Daily Bible Reading

January 1
Genesis 1:1-2:3

January 2
Genesis 2:4-25

January 3
Genesis 3

January 4
Genesis 4:1-16

January 5
Psalm 1

January 6
Romans 8:3-19

January 7
Matthew 3:13-17

January 8
Genesis 7

January 9
Genesis 8

January 10
Genesis 9:1-17

January 11
Genesis 11:1-9

January 12
Psalm 46

January 13
Proverbs 2:1-15

January 14
Colossians 3:9-17

January 15
Genesis 12:1-9

January 16
Genesis 12:10-20

January 17
Genesis 13:1-13

January 18
Genesis 15:1-21

January 19
Psalm 49:1-9

January 20
Proverbs 3:1-26

January 21
Genesis 18:1-15

January 22
Genesis 18:16-33

January 23
Genesis 19:12-26

January 24
Genesis 22:1-19

January 25
Genesis 24

January 26
Psalm 14

January 27
Proverbs 10:1-10

January 28
Genesis 25:27-34

January 29
Genesis 26:1-6

January 30
Genesis 26:17-34

January 31
Genesis 27

February 1
Proverbs 10:11-21

February 2
Genesis 29:1-30

February 3
Genesis 32

February 4
Genesis 33

February 5
Psalm 16

February 6
Proverbs 10:22-32

February 7
Genesis 37:1-11

February 8
Genesis 37:12-36

February 9
Genesis 39:1-6

February 10
Genesis 39:7-23

February 11
Psalm 18:25-34

February 12
Romans 13:1-7

February 13
1 Corinthians 13

February 14
Genesis 41:14-40

February 15
Genesis 41:41-49

February 16
Genesis 41:53-57

February 17
Genesis 42

February 18
Psalm 15

February 19
Proverbs 11:1-9

February 20
Proverbs 11:10-21

February 21
Titus 3:1-8

February 22
Genesis 45:1-16

February 23
Genesis 45:17-28

February 24
Exodus 1:15-22

February 25
Exodus 2:1-9

February 26
Exodus 2:10-22

February 27
Psalm 40

February 28
Isaiah 58:10-14

March 1
Proverbs 11:22-31

March 2
Exodus 3:1-15

March 3
Psalm 19

March 4
Proverbs 12:1-4

March 5
Exodus 4:1-17

March 6
Exodus 5

March 7
Exodus 6-7:14

March 8
Exodus 7:15-24

March 9
Exodus 8

March 10
Exodus 9

March 11
Exodus 10

March 12
Psalm 23

March 13
Proverbs 12:15-28

March 14
Exodus 12:1-28

March 15
Exodus 12:29-42

March 16
Psalm 25

March 17
Proverbs 13:1-12

March 18
Exodus 13:17-22

March 19
Exodus 14:5-14

March 20
Exodus 14:15-29

March 21
Exodus 15:1-21

March 22
Exodus 15:22-27

March 23
Exodus 16

March 24
Psalm 27

March 25
Proverbs 13:13-25

March 26 Exodus 20:1-20	**April 19** Proverbs 14:26-35	**May 13** Proverbs 16:1-16	**June 6** Psalm 85
March 27 Numbers 13:1-24	**April 20** Judges 6:11-23	**May 14** 2 Samuel 1:1-16	**June 7** Proverbs 17:1-15
March 28 Numbers 13:25-32	**April 21** Judges 6:33-40	**May 15** 2 Samuel 1:17-27	**June 8** Jonah 1
March 29 Joshua 1	**April 22** Judges 7	**May 16** 2 Samuel 5:1-16	**June 9** Jonah 2
March 30 Psalm 29	**April 23** Judges 14	**May 17** 2 Samuel 7	**June 10** Jonah 3
March 31 Proverbs 14:1-12	**April 24** Judges 16:4-21	**May 18** 2 Samuel 9	**June 11** Jonah 4
April 1 Joshua 3	**April 25** Judges 16:22-31	**May 19** 2 Samuel 22	**June 12** Daniel 3
April 2 Joshua 6	**April 26** Psalm 34:1-10	**May 20** Acts 1:1-11	**June 13** Daniel 6
April 3 Judges 6:11-23	**April 27** Proverbs 15:1-15	**May 21** 1 Kings 1:28-48	**June 14** Psalm 147
April 4 Luke 19:28-40	**April 28** 1 Samuel 1:1-20	**May 22** 1 Kings 3:1-14	**June 15** Matthew 4:1-11
April 5 Matthew 26:17-30	**April 29** 1 Samuel 1:21-28	**May 23** 1 Kings 3:15-28	**June 16** Psalm 89:5-13
April 6 Matthew 26:31-56	**April 30** 1 Samuel 2:1-10	**May 24** 1 Kings 4:29-34	**June 17** Proverbs 17:16-28
April 7 Psalm 22:19-27	**May 1** 1 Samuel 2:12-26	**May 25** Psalm 61	**June 18** John 3:1-21
April 8 Luke 22:54-62	**May 2** 1 Samuel 3	**May 26** 1 Kings 8:22-30	**June 19** John 4:4-42
April 9 Luke 23:1-25	**May 3** 1 Samuel 8:1-22	**May 27** 1 Kings 10:1-13	**June 20** Luke 6:12-19
April 10 Luke 23:33-49	**May 4** 1 Samuel 10:1-15	**May 28** 1 Kings 10:14-29	**June 21** Psalm 90
April 11 Luke 24:1-12	**May 5** 1 Samuel 10:16-27	**May 29** 1 Kings 11:1-13	**June 22** Proverbs 18:1-12
April 12 Luke 24:13-35	**May 6** 1 Samuel 15	**May 30** Psalm 84	**June 23** Matthew 5:1-12
April 13 Psalm 32	**May 7** Psalm 37:1-11	**May 31** Proverbs 16:17-33	**June 24** Matthew 5:13-26
April 14 Proverbs 14:13-25	**May 8** Proverbs 15:16-33	**June 1** Acts 1:12-26	**June 25** Matthew 5:33-48
April 15 John 20:24-31	**May 9** 1 Samuel 16:1-13	**June 2** Acts 2:1-13	**June 26** Matthew 6:1-15
April 16 John 21:1-7	**May 10** 1 Samuel 17	**June 3** Acts 2:14-43	**June 27** Matthew 6:25-34
April 17 John 21:15-25	**May 11** 1 Samuel 18:1-16	**June 4** 1 Kings 11:26-40	**June 28** Matthew 7:1-12
April 18 Psalm 33	**May 12** Psalm 51:1-13	**June 5** 1 Kings 17:8-16	**June 29** Matthew 7:13-29